A WEEKEND IN SEPTEMBER

A Weekend
In September

By JOHN EDWARD WEEMS

Illustrated with Photographs

 **Texas A&M University Press**
COLLEGE STATION

Eleventh printing, 2008

Library of Congress Cataloging-in-Publication Data

Weems, John Edward.
    A weekend in September.

    Reprint of the 1957 ed. published by Holt, New York.
    1. Galveston—Storm, 1900. I. Title.
[F394.G2W4   1980]   976.4'139   79-7415
ISBN 0-89096-097-6
ISBN 0-89096-390-8 (pbk.)
ISBN 13: 978-0-89096-390-6 (pbk.)

Manufactured in the United States of America

To Mary E. Homeyer

Foreword

SEPTEMBER 8, 1900, was a stormy Saturday in Central Texas. On a farm east of Temple the arrival of a baby was near. The family doctor was in town—ten miles away. There was no telephone.

In the afternoon a neighbor saddled his horse and left to summon the doctor. Ten miles he rode through a lashing rain that made the black Bell County soil a quagmire . . . through a wind that was felling small trees. After two and one-half hours he reached Temple.

The doctor left his home as soon as he was informed of the expected birth. Traveling on horseback, he arrived at the farmhouse in time to deliver the baby that night. Then he found himself marooned for two days by flooded creeks.

The baby, Gale, was named for the storm, and, although I never saw her, she was my aunt. She was given her life on September 8, 1900, while 205 miles to the southeast—on an island not quite thirty miles long and only three miles across at its widest point—thousands were losing their lives in what remains to this day the worst recorded disaster ever to strike the North American Continent.

Contents

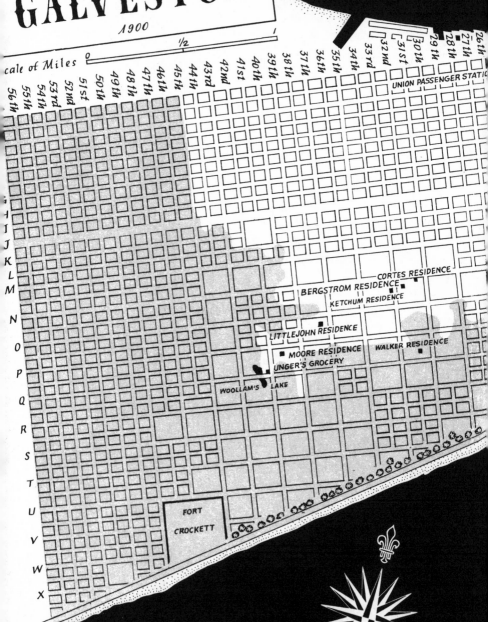

GALVESTON

1900

Scale of Miles

Galveston

UNION PASSENGER STATION

CORTES RESIDENCE

BERGSTROM RESIDENCE

KETCHUM RESIDENCE

LITTLEJOHN RESIDENCE

WALKER RESIDENCE

MOORE RESIDENCE

UNGER'S GROCERY

WOOLLAM'S LAKE

FORT CROCKETT

26th
27th
28th
29th
30th
31st
32nd
33rd
34th
35th
36th
37th
38th
39th
40th
41st
42nd
43rd
44th
45th
46th
47th
48th
49th
50th
51st
52nd
53rd
54th
55th
56th

H
I
J
K
L
M
N
O
P
Q
R
S
T
U
V
W
X

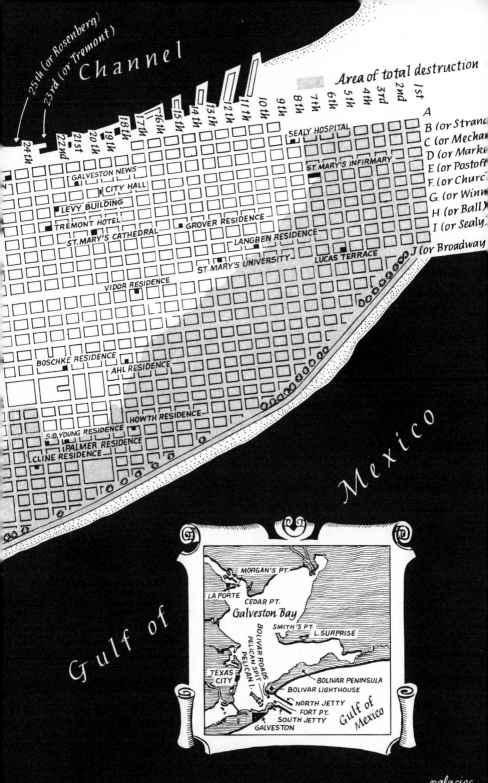

Channel

25th (or Rosenberg)
23rd (or Tremont)

Area of total destruction

1st
2nd
3rd
4th
5th
6th
7th
8th
9th
10th
11th
12th
13th
14th
15th
16th
17th
18th
19th
20th
21st
22nd
24th

SEALY HOSPITAL
ST. MARY'S INFIRMARY

A
B (or Strand
C (or Mechan
D (or Marke
E (or Postoff
F. (or Churc
G. (or Winn
H (or Ball)
I (or Sealy

J (or Broadway

GALVESTON NEWS
CITY HALL
LEVY BUILDING
TREMONT HOTEL
ST. MARY'S CATHEDRAL
GROVER RESIDENCE
LANGBEN RESIDENCE
ST. MARY'S UNIVERSITY
LUCAS TERRACE
VIDOR RESIDENCE

BOSCHKE RESIDENCE
AHL RESIDENCE

HOWTH RESIDENCE
S.O. YOUNG RESIDENCE
PALMER RESIDENCE
CLINE RESIDENCE

Gulf of

Mexico

MORGAN'S PT.
LA PORTE
CEDAR PT.
Galveston Bay
SMITH'S PT.
L. SURPRISE
BOLIVAR ROADS
PELICAN SPIT
PELICAN I.
TEXAS CITY
BOLIVAR PENINSULA
BOLIVAR LIGHTHOUSE
NORTH JETTY
FORT PT.
SOUTH JETTY
GALVESTON
Gulf of Mexico

palacios

A WEEKEND IN SEPTEMBER

1

Another Tropical Storm

THUNDERING WAVES beat against the Galveston beach. Daisy Thorne, a pretty schoolteacher whose glowing, reddish-gold hair was indicative of her spirit, watched them and decided she would not go bathing in the Gulf this Friday evening, September 7, 1900. The time was shortly after 6:30 P.M. The sun had just set, but Miss Thorne did not see it; she saw only clouds, which blotted most of the sky from her vision.

At the moment she made her decision to stay out of the water, Isaac M. Cline, local forecast official of the Galveston Weather Bureau office, was standing on the roof of the Levy Building downtown, scanning the heavens anxiously for a "brick-dust" hue, which frequently heralds the approach of a tropical hurricane. Isaac's brother, Joseph L. Cline, sat at a desk in the Weather Bureau office—on the third floor of the Levy Building—occasionally answering telephone callers who asked for information about a storm reported near the city.

Daisy Thorne usually ended her summer day with a dip —actually there was little swimming to it—in the warm Gulf waters only four blocks from her apartment. In 1900 young ladies, and particularly young red-haired

3

ladies with sensitive complexions, did not bathe in the middle of the day when the sun was fiercest—not even with those voluminous bathing suits then the fashion. Miss Thorne and her young lady friends yearned for a lily-white skin, and the midday sun, magnified in intensity by myriad reflections from an ordinarily blue-green Gulf of Mexico, could burn faces and arms in a short time. So Miss Thorne waited until early evening to go in the water, and she delighted in feeling the cool, fine sand— nearly as hard as an asphalt pavement—under her feet. There was not a better beach anywhere than Galveston's, she was sure.

But this evening's dip would have to be postponed until tomorrow. The waves were too high, and they were ugly brown with the sand they kicked up. Miss Thorne saw that nobody else was swimming either. In fact, as dusk approached, the beach was deserted except for a few persons gazing out over the turbulent water.

Miss Thorne returned to her home in flat Number 5 in Lucas Terrace, a sturdy three-story building on the northwest corner of Broadway and Sixth—at the eastern extremity of the city. She lived there with her mother, a widow; her sister, who was out of town; her brother, and a maiden aunt.

These were Daisy Thorne's last few weeks of vacation. In twenty-four days she would go back to teaching seventh-grade history, English, and drawing at Rosenberg School seven blocks away. It was an easy bicycling distance, and Miss Thorne loved to ride a bicycle; she had owned the first one with pneumatic tires in the city.

Although the twenty-three-year-old teacher soon would have much less time of her own, she was not entirely sorry to see school begin. During the coming year she would be paid fifty-five dollars a month, an increase of five dollars monthly having been granted in 1899. And she enjoyed teaching; she had taught for three years now since her graduation from Sam Houston Normal Institute in Huntsville, where she had completed a three-year course in one year. She was said to be the only person appointed to teach in Galveston schools who had not been required to serve first as a substitute. But this was to be her last year of school work. She was to be married in June to Dr. Joe Gilbert of Austin.

The summer of 1900 had not been entirely a vacation for Daisy Thorne. A good part of it had been spent making school clothes for the fall and winter. She sewed for the rest of the family too, and she helped her mother cook on their wood stove, the kind of stove most Galvestonians had. But when she was not engaged in these chores she might have been found bathing in the Gulf; or bicycling, dressed in a long, wool skirt and shirtwaist, with a veil to protect her face from the sun; or playing the piano in the parlor on the second floor; or—that summer of 1900—reading *The Love Letters of Robert Browning and Elizabeth Barrett Browning,* given to her by Dr. Gilbert.

The book was only one of many that her fiancé had sent her. After Dr. Gilbert read a book that he particularly enjoyed he always mailed it to her. Many of the volumes now were in the bookcases on each side of the fireplace in her mother's bedroom.

Miss Thorne had met Gilbert, then a medical student, in 1896, at a sailing party on Galveston Bay to which both had been invited. She was stepping from a wharf into a pitching yacht at the time. She slipped and fell into Gilbert, almost knocking him down. He helped the young lady to regain her balance in the yacht, and stayed at her side the rest of that day. Later, when refreshments were served, Miss Thorne spilled ice cream on his trousers.

Gilbert had found the young lady unforgettable. During the next year, while she was at Sam Houston Normal, the two had corresponded. In late December of 1897 they had become engaged.

During the summer of 1900 Miss Thorne also had been modeling for Mrs. J. P. McCauley, a neighbor in Lucas Terrace. Mrs. McCauley was doing a painting of a woodland nymph, and she considered Miss Thorne's five-foot-four-inch height, 113-pound weight, blue-gray eyes, and long reddish-gold hair, worn with a loose knot in the back, perfect for the nymph. However, before Mrs. Thorne had let her daughter pose she had elicited a promise from Mrs. McCauley not to paint in Daisy's face.

School was to start October 1 and end all this, but that was more than three weeks away. Miss Thorne intended to make the most of the time left.

Although Isaac and Joseph Cline were aware of the approaching storm—reported first over the Carribbean, then over the Gulf—neither man was by any means alarmed; tropical hurricanes were familiar to the two Clines and to every other resident of Galveston. If the Cline brothers were more concerned about the disturbance than other Galvestonians who knew that storm warnings were up, it was because the weather was the Clines' chief interest.

Certainly Isaac Cline had no reason to become alarmed by the threat of a storm. He lived in a well-built house four blocks from the beach, in the southern part of the city. When he built the house, on a lot 5.2 feet above sea level, he saw to it that the two-story frame structure was designed to withstand the worst Gulf storm he could imagine—and he had been in the weather service for eighteen years, eleven in Galveston. Furthermore, his house was raised above the ground, as were virtually all other houses in the city, so that its first floor was above the highwater mark of Galveston's most recent big "overflow," a hurricane that struck the city in 1875 and brought a storm tide of 8.2 feet.

Isaac Cline, still slim and physically fit at thirty-eight, was as methodical in living as he was in building his house. He divided every weekday into eight hours each of sleep, work, and recreation, but the latter was not all play. He counted as recreation such pursuits as studying the effects of weather changes on persons suffering from various diseases, lecturing in medical climatology at the University of Texas Medical College in Galveston, and—this work had been completed several years earlier—studying for the doctor of medicine degree at the University of Arkansas and the doctor of philosophy degree at Add-Ran University, now Texas Christian University of Fort Worth.

Galveston was Isaac Cline's fourth station since he had joined the Weather Bureau in 1882, when it was part of the U. S. Army's Signal Corps. While he had been in charge of the weather observation station at Abilene, in arid West Texas, he had met Cora May Ballew and married her. Now there were three daughters, Allie May, twelve; Rosemary, eleven; and Esther Ballew, six.

Joseph Cline, a twenty-nine-year-old bachelor, rented a room in his brother's house. He, too, had earned a doctor of philosophy degree from Add-Ran University. Before that, in 1892, he had come to Galveston from the family home in Monroe County, Tennessee, as a drummer at sixty dollars a month, leaving a less profitable teaching job after one year. Later in 1892 he had given up sales work for the position of assistant weather observer in his brother's office. A nondrinker in a city where liquor flowed, Joseph Cline was nevertheless popular and respected. Now—September 7, 1900—he was still on his brother's staff, as chief clerk.

An exceptionally heavy work load had kept Joseph and Isaac Cline away from the house much of the time during the first week in September, and it had prohibited the hunting and fishing trips that they both enjoyed. They were ardent hunters for wild geese and ducks that flocked to the area, and they loved to hook trout and redfish that fed in the shallow inlets around Galveston Bay. But in these first few days of September the two Clines had numerous reports to prepare on the August weather, and Isaac Cline was writing letters to several negligent volunteer weather observers inland—one had not been heard from in twenty-three months—asking them once more to submit weather reports regularly or to return the Weather Bureau's instruments.

The first advisory of a hurricane approaching the southeastern United States had reached Isaac Cline about 4:00 P.M. Tuesday, September 4, when the Weather Bureau's central office in Washington, D.C., telegraphed a terse message: "Tropical storm disturbance moving northward over Cuba."

There were no details. One reason for their absence was that in 1900 information about a tropical hurricane was not easily obtained. There were no reports radioed from ships at sea, where the storms were, and certainly there were no hurricane-hunting planes that kept watch over a tropical disturbance. Not until December 3, 1905, was a weather observation radioed from a ship—the SS *New York*—and received by the United States Weather Bureau, and not until August 26, 1909, was a hurricane report radioed—from the SS *Cartago* off the Yucatan coast. In 1900 the Weather Bureau was forced to rely on information from its stations ashore, in the United States and on Caribbean islands, for its hurricane forecasting. If the disturbance was far out at sea, it was in a blind spot as far as the central office was concerned, and the central office had sole authority to issue storm warnings.

Isaac Cline did not know until later that, although he had read the first advisory on the hurricane September 4, the storm actually had been engendered in the waning days of August, about 5000 miles from Galveston. Somewhere on the Atlantic, between South America and Africa in the easterly trades (to the north of the doldrums), water had reached a minimum temperature of 81 degrees; conditions at high levels—40,000 to 60,000 feet—had permitted evacuation of rising warm air from near the surface of the tepid ocean; and the easterly flow of the trade wind in this area had been disturbed somehow. Under these conditions the hurricane had been conceived, but Cline did not know then that a tropical cyclone was formed this way; and even today the details of origin are not fully comprehended.

Cline also was unaware at the time that the threat of this particular storm had first been observed on August 30, when the disturbance was reported in the vicinity of latitude 15 degrees north, longitude 63 west. This was about 125 miles northwest of Martinique, a small French-held island in the Windward chain, 1500 miles southeast of Miami.

As the weak cyclonic disturbance passed the area, several severe thunderstorms raked islands in the Windward and Leeward group. One was particularly bad on Antigua. The Antigua *Standard,* observing that "a burnt child dreads the fire," commented on the alarm caused by the weather advisory about the disturbance.

"The lowering appearance of the heavens, anon tinged with a strange yellow light, an ominous stillness and intense heat, and withal a falling barometer, tended to increase the fear," it reported, in the flowery journalistic style then popular. "In the early evening distant vivid flashes of lightning in the north and east presaged a thunderstorm which gradually approached us."

The signal station flagstaff on Antigua's Goat Hill was splintered by lightning, and it crashed to the ground. Telephone posts and lines on the island were damaged.

After that the disturbance had moved almost due west in the Caribbean. On the morning of August 31 it was 200 miles south of Puerto Rico. At 8:00 A.M., September 1, it was 200 miles south of Santo Domingo City—now Ciudad Trujillo, capital of the Dominican Republic—and it had acquired all the characteristics of a tropical hurricane.

As it traveled, at about fifteen miles an hour, its diameter expanded. Winds becoming increasingly violent were blowing counterclockwise around a low-pressure center about ten miles in diameter. Over a large area of the Caribbean only this center was relatively windless. But on the surface of the sea, inside that calm area, the water was extremely rough. The towering waves would have badly battered and perhaps sunk a vessel caught in their grasp. Outside the calm area, wind blew away the tops of waves in sheets of spray.

At eight o'clock on the morning of Sunday, September 2, the storm was 200 miles south of Haiti; it was still

moving westward. Had it continued moving in this direction, it would have struck a point between Nicaragua and
Mexico's Yucatan Peninsula; but the storm turned north,
toward Cuba. On the morning of September 3 it was 175
miles south of the mid-section of that island; by 8:00
A.M., September 4, it was just south of Cuba.

Later this same day Isaac Cline had read the first advisory, the one that said a tropical storm disturbance was
moving northward over Cuba. Until September 4 the
storm had not developed a really destructive force, although it did cause rough seas and heavy rains. Clouds
had dumped twelve and a half inches of water in twenty-
four hours as they passed over Santiago, Cuba; more than
ten inches of that amount fell in eight hours.

After Tuesday, September 4, Cline had been regularly
informed of the storm's progress. On Wednesday morning,
September 5, the hurricane, then 900 miles southeast of
Galveston, was traveling almost due north, evidently aim-
ing a blow at Florida. At 10:20 A.M. that day Isaac Cline
had received and distributed a second advisory from
Washington: "Disturbance central near Key West moving northwest. Vessels bound for Florida and Cuban
ports should exercise caution as the storm is likely to become dangerous."

On Thursday, September 6, Cline was informed that
the center was a short distance northwest of Key West;
late that evening telegraph wires were broken south of
Jacksonville, and some wires between Pensacola and
Jacksonville went down. The central office ordered storm
and hurricane warnings up from Port Eads, Louisiana, on
the Gulf, to Hatteras, on the Atlantic, and advisory messages were being issued along the East Coast as far north
as Boston.

But Boston need not have worried, for on Thursday the storm had begun moving almost due west again; and on Friday morning, September 7, the center was southeast of the Louisiana coast.

At 9:35 A.M., Friday, the storm warnings were extended to Galveston. Isaac Cline received notification of this fifty-five minutes later, and by 10:35 A.M. he had hoisted two weather signals, which flapped in a seventeen-mile-an-hour north wind on a pole atop the Levy Building. Most people in Galveston who saw them knew that the red flag with a black center meant that a storm of marked violence was expected. Above the flag the people saw a white pennant; the storm wind would come from the northwest. The central office thus had predicted that the vortex of the hurricane would strike the coast somewhere to the east of Galveston. Cline knew what this probably would mean: the city would be comparatively safe, because it would be on the storm's left as it crossed the coastline. Isaac Cline knew from experience that areas in the left semicircle seemed to suffer much less damage.

Friday morning he had noticed the first sign of an approaching tropical storm: an increasing swell coming from the southeast. Later he had observed the second sign: delicate wisps of cirrus clouds, making the blue sky seem a canvas on which a painter had hurriedly brushed thin streaks of white. They, too, came from the southeast, only a few at first. But to Cline these cirrus were the harbingers of more clouds to come; soon the sky would be overcast.

Now, Friday evening, shortly after the time of sunset—while Daisy Thorne was on the beach deciding against the dip—Isaac Cline was out looking for the "brick-dust" sky. Some of the red hue in this phenomenon might be caused by smoke or dust, but moisture intensifies the color, so that the whole sky just after sunset is crimson; it seems the heavens are aflame.

Cline's meteorological predecessors, even with their much more limited knowledge of the weather, had recognized as far back as biblical times the portent of what he called a "brick-dust" sky; but many of them obviously believed it was ominous only in the morning, for the sixteenth chapter of Matthew contains these verses:

"He answered and said unto them, When it is evening, ye say, It will be fair weather: for the sky is red.

"And in the morning, It will be foul weather today: for the sky is red and lowring . . . "

William Shakespeare also wrote about it:

A red morn, that ever yet betoken'd
Wrack to the seamen, tempest to the field,
Sorrow to shepherds, woe unto the birds,
Gusts and foul flaws to herdmen and to herds.

But Cline did not see a "brick-dust" sky. He saw instead that the morning cirrus had indeed heralded the arrival of more clouds. The sky seemed to him to be nearly covered with thick rolls of strato-cumulus. They were coming, he observed, from the northeast.

Below Isaac Cline, on the third floor of the building, Joseph Cline would soon turn over the job of answering telephone calls to another meteorologist, on temporary duty at Galveston, and he would join his brother on the roof, where most of the weather instruments were, to take the evening readings.

While the Cline brothers were thus occupied, the family of Police Chief Edwin N. Ketchum—Mr. and Mrs.

Ketchum and eight children—were halfway through the evening meal.

They lived on the west side of the city, in a two-story Colonial house built in 1838 by the founder of Galveston, Michel B. Menard. It was erected only seventeen years after the pirate, Jean Lafitte, had been ordered off Galveston Island by the United States. Sixty-two years of weathering Gulf blows had left it in a condition just as good as when it was built from wood brought on sailing vessels. The center section was framed in Maine white pine; sills were made from Georgia and Florida pine. The entire house was mortised. Joists were set with white lead.

Ketchum had bought the house in 1880. Now, twenty years later, he was police chief of Galveston; he had made his twenty-year-old son, Henry, responsible for running his general contracting business.

Ed Ketchum—tall, slender, and personable—was a popular chief despite the fact that he had fought the Civil War as drummer boy and, later, as captain on the Union side; Galveston was a hotbed of Confederate veterans. But Ketchum was respected; he was honest, and he played no favorites.

A man's wife might come to Chief Ketchum at police headquarters and tell him that her husband had lost so much money gambling that she and her children were starving. The chief then would go to the gambler who had taken the money and explain the situation.

"Just a minute, Ed," the man would usually say, and he would go to the safe. When he returned it was with the amount of money the husband had lost.

"Don't let that man in your place again," Ketchum would request. It was as good as an order.

Another story attested to the chief's popularity. Ketchum owned a large coffee urn that was the envy of quite a few Galvestonians. When groups of Confederate veterans got together for reunions or meetings they borrowed it.

"We hate to borrow it from a Union soldier," a Southerner told Ketchum once, "but you're the best damn Yankee we've ever known."

Ketchum had returned to the city Tuesday, September 4, from an encampment of the Grand Army of the Republic in Chicago. Like the Clines, he had been especially busy during the rest of the week, disposing of work that had piled up in his absence. The day he returned from Chicago he had seen the first advisory of the storm, when it was moving northward over Cuba, and he too had read the advisories after that. At supper Friday evening Ketchum mentioned briefly the storm warning, and a forecast Isaac Cline had released earlier Friday calling for increasing north winds during the night. But the wind was light—about eleven miles an hour—as the Ketchums were at their supper, and the police chief supposed that if the storm did hit it would not be very bad.

Ten blocks from the Ketchums, Mr. and Mrs. Ephraim Moore and six children also were at supper. (One son, living with his grandmother, was not present.) Moore worked for a downtown grocery store; his job was to make the rounds of customers' houses, to take orders for groceries, and to deliver them in his wagon, collecting the money upon delivery.

For two days now Ephraim Moore had been hearing reports of the storm, but he paid little attention to them. He was by nature a calm man; his unimposing physical size —five-foot-eight, 145 pounds—was more than compensated for by a quiet self-assurance. Besides, he had been in Galveston all his life and had been through several tropical hurricanes. Moore had seen his city weather them all, although other towns on the Texas coast had been badly damaged by storms. (Indianola, farther south down the coast, was destroyed by a hurricane on August 20, 1886; the town never did rebuild.)

The Moore family, too, mentioned the storm that was forecast to blow in that night, but they talked about it only briefly. It was just another tropical storm to them.

Thirteen-year-old Jim Moore, a freckle-faced youngster, was much more concerned about the approaching opening of school, but he kept this dreary thought private. As Jim ate his soup—often served for supper at the Moore residence—he realized sadly that in about three weeks he would be in the high third grade at Alamo School, and that this would certainly bring to an abrupt end his carefree summer days of playing baseball with his young friends in the vacant lot behind his house, of playing with his new black puppy, and of seining and swimming in the Gulf.

Although the thought of school clouded Jim Moore's Friday somewhat, Walter Grover, an employee of a downtown real estate firm, thought that the day had been beautiful. The afternoon had been exceptionally hot for Galveston—91 degrees—but Grover was in his office at H. M. Trueheart and Company when the thermometer registered that maximum, and the heat did not bother him much. Walking home from work along palm- and oleander-lined streets, he had been cooled by a gentle north breeze.

Grover did not mind these walks to and from work; in

fact he enjoyed them. He ignored the electric streetcars that ran in front of his house on Winnie—he lived there with his father and mother—and always walked. (The only other alternative was to ride a wagon or buggy; there were only one or two automobiles in the city.) Grover was not trying to avoid paying the nickel fare; he simply wanted to be outdoors, where he could observe the life around him.

An insatiable curiosity was perhaps the outstanding characteristic of Grover, a tall, slender, thirty-one-year-old man in excellent health. It was responsible for his knowing at least as much and perhaps more about the Galveston area than anyone else in the city. He was familiar with all of Galveston Island, stretching from southwest to northeast along the Texas coast, from San Luis Pass at its western tip to the city of Galveston (and Fort Point) at its eastern extremity. Grover even knew exactly where the highest point on the whole island was—at its mid-section, where the sand had formed a rise to a point about fifteen feet above water. (The highest ground in the city itself was on Broadway, 8.7 feet above the Gulf.) He had spent many hours, in his younger days, investigating the tall sand dunes along the Gulf beach, on the south side of the island. But by 1900 many of these dunes had been removed, the sand having been used to fill in low areas.

Grover also enjoyed exploring expansive Galveston Bay, to the north of the island, in a small sailboat. On these expeditions he hunted, fished, camped, and studied bird life. He became so proficient in handling boats in the area that he was given a pilot's license to navigate small steamers in the bay.

Earlier in life he had found his first adventures in several ways. One was by tying a string between trees on opposite sides of a walk and listening to the oaths of passing gentlemen when their beavers were knocked off. Walter and his young friends also amused themselves by making rat-shaped objects out of the Spanish moss that abounded in Galveston; they would tie a long string to one of these "rats," put the object in the grass near a walk, and hide behind a nearby shrub, across the walk, holding the other end of the string. A scampering rat would always scare the ladies, and it usually startled their male escorts also.

"In those days men always wore beavers and carried canes," Walter Grover remembers now. "I don't know how many canes were broken on those moss rats."

Grover had grown up with an intense love for his city. In 1900 he was, as were most other Galvestonians, proud of its importance. The state's fourth largest city, it had more than 37,000 residents. They represented many races, for Galveston's population was cosmopolitan. It was the wealthiest city per capita in the whole Southwest. In fact, among United States cities of its size only Providence, Rhode Island, had more money. Galveston was a vacation resort, offering everything from gambling and a red-light district, for those who were looking for a fling, to restaurants with excellent cuisine, picturesque picnicking spots, and musical concerts. It was a booming seaport, which had forty-four steamship offices; a commercial center, from which drummers went to places as far inland as New Mexico and the Indian Territory seeking customers.

But Grover was also quite aware of the fact that Galveston was a city built on sand, and from his explorations he knew that it was not a very large pile at that. This was, however, far from his thoughts Friday evening, September 7. Reaching home after the eleven-block walk from his office, Grover went inside his house briefly; then he reappeared on the front gallery. He sat down in a chair to relax for a few minutes before the call to supper came. While he waited, he noticed once more the north wind. He was glad that it was brisk enough to offer relief from the unusually warm evening.

2 FRIDAY, SEPTEMBER 7

Northerly Winds on the Coast

OTHER GALVESTONIANS besides Daisy Thorne and the two Clines became aware of an increasing surf roar; many of them, like the Ketchums and Moores, mentioned the storm warning in conversations during the day but dismissed it after a brief reference. Most of them, like Walter Grover, thought Friday was a nice day, although a bit too hot. (And there were more than a few persons in the city who were entirely unaware of the storm warning.)

Captain J. W. Simmons of the steamship *Pensacola* had read the hurricane advisories, including the one Isaac Cline received Wednesday, warning vessels bound for Cuban and Florida ports to exercise caution. But Friday was Simmons' sailing date, and at 7:00 A.M. he got under way from Pier 34—at 34th Street—bound for Pensacola, Florida.

Weather conditions seemed good enough to Simmons, although he thought it was warm, especially for so early in the morning. While getting the ship away from its pier he exchanged a few words from time to time with his guest for this voyage, Galveston pilot commissioner J. M. O. Menard, who was also on the bridge.

When the *Pensacola* was in the channel, heading east-

ward, Simmons mopped his forehead with a rumpled handkerchief and saw that his was the only ship under way.
(No other steamer sailed during the rest of Friday either.)
A few miles astern of the *Pensacola* were a two-mile-long
wagon bridge and three railroad bridges, close together,
which connected Galveston Island with Virginia Point on
the mainland. On the starboard quarter was a 200-acre
area on which the Southern Pacific Railway was building
a giant terminal to link its railroad with the sea. Close by
to starboard, the two- and three-story brick buildings of
downtown Galveston seemed to be moving slowly past
Simmons' ship; he could see the top of the large, five-story
Tremont Hotel—called by many persons the finest hotel
south of Saint Louis—five blocks farther in from the
wharf front. (The first floors of these downtown buildings also were raised several feet off the ground as a protection against "overflows.") On the *Pensacola's* port side,
as she steamed past the downtown area, was a mound of
sand known as Pelican Island.

The ship gained speed, and the buildings went past
more quickly; before long they were gone, and to starboard was Fort Point, on the eastern tip of Galveston Island. Simmons could see here Fort San Jacinto, its guns
seemingly poking out of sand; the quarantine station, built
on pilings that raised it more than six feet above the
ground; and Fort Point Lighthouse, about sixty feet
high. Then the *Pensacola* turned to starboard, passed several ships anchored in Bolivar Roads, and steamed into
the open Gulf between two jetties. One, called the south
jetty, extended southeastward from Fort Point. The north
jetty was parallel to it, projecting from the tip of Bolivar
Peninsula, on the mainland about two miles away. The
jetties had been constructed by the federal government in

a recent 8,500,000-dollar program to improve Galveston's harbor facilities; they served to deepen the channel.

When Simmons reached the open Gulf he ordered the *Pensacola* on a more easterly course, logged the wind as fresh—nineteen to twenty-four miles an hour—and went below to his cabin, with Menard, to relax.

Attorney Clarence Howth was also taking his ease at this time Friday morning, if that could be said of a man about to become a father. He was sitting in the parlor of his two-story house three blocks from the beach, reading the morning Galveston *News* while he smoked a cigar.

Howth had bought the house seven years earlier because of his love for the nearby beach. He had enjoyed every year of residence since then, and the summer of 1900 had been especially delightful to him; he thought of it as "one long, pleasant dream under the shade trees."

His wife's first baby was due in September. Howth thought that he should stay home from the office that day because the arrival seemed imminent. During the morning hours he was solicitous for his wife's comfort; frequently he went upstairs to her bedroom to ask how she was. But about 8:30 A.M. he found time to read the morning edition of the *News*.

Page one, he saw, was devoted largely to the Boxer Rebellion, which had flamed into open warfare in June. The rebellion was named for a Chinese political society dedicated to the expulsion of foreigners from the country. By August 14 the foreign allies had captured Peking, the Chinese capital; Howth read in his September 7 newspaper a dispatch sent August 28 from Peking describing the entry of allied forces—including some United States troops—into the palace grounds. The palace was vacant except for some 300 servants.

Turning to page two, he read a story that brought to the fore his civic pride. Datelined Washington, September 6, the item reported the 1900 census figures for Galveston. The city had grown from a population of 29,084 in 1890 to 37,789; total for the United States was 75,578,-000, the census bureau estimated.

Howth read each page in detail; on most weekday mornings he did not have this much time for the paper. He particularly enjoyed several long stories on the coming presidential election pitting William Jennings Bryan against William McKinley. (The Galveston *News* was supporting McKinley.)

Howth read news items on seven pages of the paper before he came to the local weather story, on page eight. There the official weather forecast, which always came from Washington, occupied about one inch of space in column two. For eastern Texas partly cloudy weather was predicted for Friday, "with showers and cooler on the coast." For Saturday fair weather was foreseen, accompanied by "fresh, possibly brisk, northerly winds on the coast." Immediately below the weather forecast Howth read a small headline in bold-face type.

"Tropical Storm Movement," it announced. Also datelined Washington, it was a message to the weather observer at Galveston, describing the tropical storm centered over southern Florida and moving slowly northward. The wind at Jupiter, on the east coast of Florida, was forty-eight miles an hour from the east, Howth read. The wind on Georgia and South Carolina coasts was freshening. "The center will move slowly northward," the item ended.

By that Friday morning, of course, this news was already outdated; for the storm was now moving westward in the Gulf of Mexico, but Howth did not know it. He barely noticed the daily barometric readings; at 7:00 A.M., September 6, the day before, the Galveston barometer was 29.974. The 7:00 P.M. reading was slightly lower. (The barometer kept falling slowly but consistently after that.)

Howth skimmed the next two pages—nothing much of interest to him there—and put down the paper. He crushed out the cigar in an ashtray; then he went upstairs again to see about his wife.

Even as Howth read the morning paper, part of the Galveston *News* staff was working on Saturday's edition. There were ten pages to fill. Ads were light; most space would go to news.

In the summer of 1900 many of the telegraph stories not on the subject of the Boxer Rebellion or the presidential election concerned Carrie Nation, the Kansas antisaloon agitator, who was raiding bars with a hatchet; the question of when the twentieth century began—not until January 1, 1901, said Vatican officials and some other authorities (and since Galveston was largely Catholic, this statement was generally accepted); heavyweight boxing champion James J. Jeffries; and the work begun by Doctors Walter Reed, Aristides Agramonte, Jesse Lazear, and James Carroll to wipe out yellow fever.

The *News* editor was interested in this medical work, as were many others in the city. Galveston had been plagued by yellow fever through the years since its charter of incorporation was granted in 1839. Of the 1000 residents, 250 died of the disease that same year. In 1844 more than 3500 persons had it, and 400 succumbed. In

1867 the epidemic was so bad that authorities stopped tolling the bell atop Saint Mary's Cathedral for a yellow fever victim. The bell was ringing constantly; 1150 of 18,000 died. In those days Galveston had just one major defense against the disease: chinking cracks in the north side of the house. If a north wind should hit a yellow fever patient, people believed, he would keel over like a wilted flower and die.

The *News* editor had scheduled only a few local stories for the next edition. The most important of these was a Friday morning interview with the city engineer, R. H. Peek, concerning streets.

The city's streets posed a problem. Some were paved with wood blocks brought in years earlier as ships' ballast. A few others were covered with shells, but the white shell caused such a glare that many persons had to close the shutters in midday. Many other streets were just sand, as nature had made them. For although Galveston was a wealthy city, the municipal government was in poor financial condition, and there was little money to spend on civic projects. But something had to be done.

What about paving with macadam? Peek told the reporter that morning that he was not in favor of it; he did not think that it would stand "the wear and tear." It was not heavy traffic or weight that wore out macadam, the city engineer declared, but the horses that stood in one place while they were tethered, and made holes in the pavement. The breaks would spread, he declared, and eventually ruin the surface.

The condition of the streets did not prevent Mr. and Mrs. Frank Walker from driving at noon to a restaurant on the beach for a steak dinner. Walker was composing-room foreman at a stationery firm; the couple lived on the south side of the city, seven blocks from the beach.

Mrs. Walker still remembers how the crashing surf frightened their horse, Bess, so badly that they hurried their meal to get back to her before she broke the reins and trotted off with the buggy. Mrs. Walker also remembers remarking on the threatening sea to the proprietress.

"Aren't you worried that the water is so rough?" Mrs. Walker inquired.

"No," the woman answered. "I like it."

By the time the Walkers had finished eating, the *Pensacola,* out in the Gulf, had run into a wind that was steadily increasing. The ship's barometer now was falling rapidly. Captain Simmons was worried.

Captains of vessels like the *Pensacola* have had reason to fear storms in this part of the world for centuries. The first European to visit the Texas interior, Cabeza de Vaca, was shipwrecked in a Gulf storm in 1528. Probably he was wrecked on Galveston Island, although some historians say it was elsewhere. Cabeza de Vaca named the island *Malhado*—"Misfortune."

The earliest recorded history of West Indian hurricanes antedates that by thirty-five years. On February 12, 1493, Christopher Columbus was nearing the Azores, bound for Spain from the West Indies, when his ships encountered what was evidently a tropical hurricane. The wind began blowing fiercely, and for several hours it seemed to increase in velocity. Then came a lull, but after that the wind blew furiously from the opposite direction.

In 1818 four ships belonging to Jean Lafitte were driven aground at Galveston. Little more than a decade later Stephen F. Austin, founder of an American colony in the

Mexican state of Texas, was riding over the flat Gulf country with a party of horsemen when they came upon a sailing vessel blown far inland from Galveston Bay. It was rotting on dry land.

"Someday," Austin is said to have observed, "the elements which did that will sweep over this coast again."

Friday afternoon Austin's observation was proving true, at least for the *Pensacola*. The ship encountered heavy seas from the east. Captain Simmons ordered his crew of twenty-one to take in awnings, to batten hatches, to make everything snug. Still the barometer fell, to 28.55. Late in the afternoon Captain Simmons summoned Menard, the pilot commissioner, who was on the bridge watching the weather.

"Menard, look at that glass," Simmons said. "I've never seen it that low. You never have and probably never will again."

A few hours later Simmons estimated the wind at hurricane force—more than seventy-five miles an hour. He dropped his anchor, with 100 fathoms of chain, in the open Gulf. The *Pensacola* swung to it but labored heavily, alternately rising and falling on tremendous seas. The noise was deafening. Cabin crockery smashed into countless pieces. A large medicine chest that had not been moved in years was thrown across the ship and landed in a bathroom. The captain's large Danish hound became seasick. To Captain Simmons this was the roughest weather he had seen in 800 trips across the Gulf.

"It seemed the ship couldn't stand the thumping for long," Pilot Commissioner Menard said afterward. "We feared she would break some bolts or strain the plates—or break in two. We would have gone down in five minutes."

Late that afternoon, while Simmons was employing all the knowledge of seamanship at his command to stay afloat, Morris Sheppard, sovereign banker of the Woodmen of the World, worked briefly in his hotel room on an address he was to make at a Woodmen meeting Saturday night. Sheppard, who later served as U. S. representative and senator from Texas for a total of thirty-eight years, was accompanied on his trip to Galveston by W. A. Fraser, state deputy organizer. The two men were staying in the Tremont Hotel.

Nearly everybody of any importance registered at the Tremont during a Galveston visit. Twenty years earlier, Ulysses Grant and Phil Sheridan, two of the most famous celebrities who came to Galveston in the nineteenth century, had also stayed there. On the night of March 24, 1880, the two former Union generals were honored guests at a banquet in the Tremont dining room. Inasmuch as General Sheridan had said, several years before, "If I owned Texas and all hell, I would rent out Texas and live in hell," there were many persons who had misgivings about this dinner. But the general came through handsomely. He arose and in a brief talk explained that he had made the statement after completing a hot and dusty stagecoach trip in the dry interior. The general added a few more words, all superlative in their praise of Texas, before he sat down. Whether or not Sheridan was sincere, many hands slapped his back in the Tremont that night in 1880.

When Morris Sheppard finished working on his address, he and Fraser went downstairs; they had supper in the same dining room where Grant and Sheridan had been honored.

While the two men were dining, Clarence Howth watered his young cauliflower plants in the back yard of his home near the beach. Earlier, he had called Mrs. Howth's physician and a nurse, and both were upstairs with her.

Many other Galvestonians besides Howth remembered years later with remarkable clarity what they had been doing that Friday evening. Mrs. W. L. Love recalls a remark made by a visitor at the house, five blocks from the beach, where her mother and grandmother lived. Mrs. Love had come to Galveston from Houston on Monday, September 3, with her five-year-old son, Sydney. Her husband, a printer in the composing room of the Houston *Daily Post,* had stayed behind; although Monday was Labor Day, it had been no holiday for him. The visitor, a priest from New Orleans, remarked that a storm was predicted to hit Galveston.

About midnight Clarence Howth heard a similar comment from the doctor. A short time earlier, while a gusty north wind was blowing, a cry heard throughout the residence had announced the arrival of the newest Howth. The physician, on his way out of the house, said to Howth that the storm, expected to hit that night, had failed to materialize. Mrs. Howth, he said, was resting well.

By the time the doctor left Clarence Howth's residence nearly all the night-side staff had left the *News* building.

Most of the space in Saturday's edition had been filled with national and international news. The telegraph editor, R. B. Spangler, had chosen for top display on page one a report from Washington on the Boxer Rebellion. It reported that a plan for withdrawing United States troops from Peking might be approved.

One reporter had written a local weather story after

consulting the Galveston Weather Bureau office. The storm, which had been playing in the South Atlantic and Caribbean for several days, he reported, had changed its course. Reaching the Gulf, it was moving northwest and would probably strike land somewhere east of Texas.

Just before midnight a staff member went outside, gazed heavenward, came back into the office, and wrote a paragraph to follow the earlier story.

"At midnight," he reported, "the moon was shining brightly and the sky was not as threatening as earlier in the night. The weather bureau had no late advices as to the storm's movements and it may be that the tropical disturbance has changed its course or spent its force before reaching Texas."

3 SATURDAY, 12:01–8:00 A.M.

Unusually Heavy Swells

CHIEF CLERK Joseph Cline had stayed late at the Weather Bureau office Friday night preparing a weather map to go to the Texas interior. When he completed it he took it to the post office, to be sure it got on the early-morning train. Then he walked to his room in his brother's house, four blocks from the beach. Exhausted, he fell into bed at one o'clock.

But he had difficulty going to sleep. His mind was on the hurricane creeping toward the city. For three hours Cline rolled and tossed fitfully. About four o'clock in the morning he arose.

"In some obscure way," he recalled later, "I sensed that the waters of the Gulf were already over our back yard."

He went to a south window of his bedroom and saw that his fear was well founded; the yard was under several inches of water. The center of the storm was still more than 200 miles southeast of Galveston, but the hurricane was causing an abnormally high tide along much of the upper Texas coast. It was this tide that was flooding the lowest areas in Galveston.

Joseph Cline woke his brother, and the two made plans for meeting the emergency. Isaac Cline said he would

31

stay on the beach to observe the tide and to warn people on the low ground to evacuate. He asked Joseph to go to the office and assemble data for a weather report to be telegraphed out of Galveston.

At five o'clock Isaac Cline made his first observation of the tide. He found that it was four and one-half feet above what it should have been, and that Gulf water already was covering the area nearest the beach, to a distance of four blocks inland in some places. (From five o'clock on, until the wires went down, the Galveston Weather Bureau office telegraphed complete observations every two hours to the central office in Washington.)

Few people had been awake when Joseph Cline first noticed sea water in his back yard. Among those few were late-leavers from the *News* building.

Telegraph editor Spangler, after seeing the paper to bed, left the editorial room about 3:45 A.M. for his home three blocks from the beach. He had read the wire stories on the storm with interest. A little after 1:00 A.M. there had come a special to the *News* from New Orleans reporting a severe storm along the Mississippi and Louisiana coastline. Most of the wires were down, the story said, and details were unavailable. Later an Associated Press dispatch confirmed the storm, but its report also lacked details.

These stories were the main reason Spangler was late leaving the office. He had stayed to see that the most recent storm news got into Saturday's edition, in a spot on page three.

It was a twenty-two-block walk to his home from the *News* building. When Spangler was two blocks away from his house he struck knee-deep water. After wading a block farther, he could see waves dashing over a railroad track that ran in front of his house. But this had happened before, and he was not particularly alarmed.

Shortly after 4:00 A.M.—fifteen minutes after Spangler left the building—George Trebosius departed from the *News* mailing room, where he was employed. He lived thirty blocks away and, instead of walking that distance, he waited for the streetcars to begin running at six o'clock. One went to within three blocks of his residence. When he reached home Trebosius, a married man for eight months now, found the Gulf waters up to his knees in his yard.

At the same time Trebosius was arriving home, S. O. Young, secretary of the Galveston Cotton Exchange, was standing near the beach, not far from the Trebosius residence, watching the rollers coming in. He had gone there at 6:00 A.M. While he watched, the tide completely covered a street railway track running along the beach.

"I was certain a cyclone was coming," Young said later. "As soon as I could I went to town and telegraphed my wife and children on a Southern Pacific train coming from the West to stop in San Antonio. I told them a storm was about to hit Galveston."

Isaac Cline was also at the beach, still observing the swells. After he had made his first observation of the tide at five o'clock he had gone to the Weather Bureau office briefly. There he had discovered that the barometer was only one-tenth of an inch lower than Friday evening's reading; then he had returned to the beach front.

A fifteen-mile-an-hour north-northwest wind was blowing against the swells, which were still coming from the southeast, Cline observed. Usually a north wind—blowing into the Gulf—caused a low tide at Galveston. ("If we had a north wind," Walter Grover remembers of the years before 1900, "you could walk halfway to Cuba.") But now, in spite of a steadily increasing north wind, the tide was continuing to rise.

Once more Isaac Cline went back to his office and filed a telegram to the central office in Washington.

"Unusually heavy swells from the southeast, intervals one to five minutes, overflowing low places south portion of city three to four blocks from beach," he stated. "Such high water with opposing winds never observed previously."

Years later Cline elaborated on his observations made early that Saturday morning:

"The storm swells were increasing in magnitude and frequency and were building up a storm tide which told me as plainly as though it was a written message that a great danger was approaching. Neither the barometer nor the winds were telling me, but the storm tide was telling me to warn the people of the danger approaching."

Cline harnessed his horse to a two-wheeled cart that he and his brother used on their frequent hunting trips, and drove up and down the beach warning residents near the Gulf to move to higher ground. To the summer tourists still in Galveston he advised: get out; go home now. His warnings were relayed along the coast.

Twelve days after the storm an editorial in the New York *Evening Sun* acclaimed Cline's work:

"The warnings which were sent out by Dr. Cline are said to have saved thousands of lives along the coast. The Texas papers show that in some towns and villages and at many plantations and farms the force of the wind and the rise of the water were necessarily fatal to life as at

Galveston, but the inhabitants and residents profited by their information and escaped inland."

Even as Cline made his Revere-like ride up and down the beach the storm tide grew worse. And while the hurricane southeast of Galveston was forcing the Gulf higher upon the south beach, the north wind was piling up water on the bay side. Nevertheless, the city would not suffer so much damage as long as the north wind held. Although it could not dissipate the swells, it kept the water lower than if the wind had been coming from the east or southeast, pushing the tide ashore.

Most other Galvestonians did not share Isaac Cline's concern about the tide, although by the time most people were awake it had already picked up several small two-wheeled bathhouses on the beach and deposited them, upside down or on their sides, a block or so inland. In the summer tourist season these bathhouses could be rented and rolled out into the water a short distance. A bather, after a swim in the Gulf, dressed and signaled the concessionaire; the man came with a horse and pulled the bathhouse ashore, saving the bather from getting sand on his feet and in his stockings and shoes.

After breakfast residents of the city began preparing for Saturday's work—in 1900 almost everybody had a six-day week. For grocery clerk Ephraim Moore it would be busier than most days. People liked to buy groceries in quantity, and the last day of the week was popular for shopping. Immediately after breakfast Moore left in his wagon for the store downtown.

At the same time, Police Chief Ketchum left his home for City Hall, and young Henry Ketchum prepared for another day of overseeing his father's general contracting business. Saturday morning meant going out with the men employed by his father—and the teams and wagons—to supervise the transfer of cotton from railroad yards to compresses.

At 7:30 A.M., as usual, Walter Grover started to walk to work. He went west on Winnie, the street on which his parents' residence was located. At 17th Street he stopped and looked toward the Gulf where "mighty big waves" were breaking on the beach. Although they were fourteen blocks away, he could see them clearly. Grover watched for a few minutes and walked on toward the office. Shortly after he arrived there a light shower dampened the streets. It was brief, but the low clouds suggested that more rain would fall soon.

About the time Grover left his house, H. M. Curtin left his summer home on Morgan's Point, on the bay some thirty miles to the north of Galveston, for work in Houston. Curtin, a real estate agent, took his family to Morgan's Point every summer, for it was much cooler there. The weather seemed threatening when Curtin left the house Saturday morning, and he carried an umbrella. On the way to nearby La Porte, where he caught a train for Houston, the umbrella collapsed in the wind. His first thought, that this was an omen and that he should return home to his wife and two children, quickly gave way to a decision that it was just a gust of wind.

Shortly before 8:00 A.M. attorney Clarence Howth left his residence for work. Having remained at home Friday with his wife, he thought that he must put in an appearance at his office downtown. Water from the Gulf had surrounded his house when he left, and he saw many of his neighbors wading to the streetcar line. A few persons occupying frail houses in the neighborhood were, he noted, packing.

They are clearly strangers, he said to himself. Vacationers. They don't realize that the Gulf is harmless.

Before eight o'clock many persons in the higher sections had heard that the low areas were flooded, but to virtually everybody in the city it was only another overflow, as the occasional storm-swept inundations were called. It would recede, they thought, within a few hours. The word spread quickly, however, that the waves were a grand sight. Galvestonians who had seen them advised their friends to go to the beach.

Mrs. Charles Vidor heard about the waves by telephone at her home in the central part of the city. Her cousin called to suggest that she take "the boys" down to the beach to see the wonderful breakers. "The boys" were Mrs. Vidor's five-year-old son, King, and two young friends visiting from Fort Worth. Mrs. Vidor's husband had already left the house for work at the Galveston Bagging and Cordage Company.

Even from a distance the towering waves made an impression on young King Vidor, who in later years was to become a well-known motion picture director.

"As we looked up the sandy street the mile to the sea," he recalled afterward, "I could see the waves crash against the streetcar trestle, then shoot into the air as high as the telephone poles. Higher. My mother didn't speak as we watched three or four waves.

"I was only five then, but I remember now that it seemed as if we were in a bowl looking up toward the level of the sea. As we stood there in the sandy street, my mother and I, I wanted to take my mother's hand and hurry her away. I felt as if the sea was going to break over the edge of the bowl and come pouring down upon us."

Mrs. Vidor took King and his friends down to the beach; they rode a streetcar. After reaching the beach, they watched the enormous waves pound several amusement houses to pieces.

"Large bathhouses were reduced to splinters," Mrs. Vidor recalls now, "and a street railway trestle over which we had just ridden was twisted and unearthed."

Then it began to rain, and Mrs. Vidor led the boys away from the beach. They hurried up 23rd Street to the home of George W. Boschke, a Southern Pacific official, where the parents of the two Fort Worth boys were staying.

Many who went to the beach did not bother to don rainy-day garb before going out. Like Mrs. Vidor and the boys, they got off the streetcars that brought them and made their way to the best vantage points through pools of water left by the thunderous breakers. Soon they were soaked by rain and spray.

The same rain that drove Mrs. Vidor and her three charges to shelter kept Mrs. W. L. Love and her grandmother, mother, and son at home. They had been planning to go to the Henry H. Morris photography studio that morning, where a four-generation picture was to be taken. After that they were to visit the home of Kate Spann, Mrs. Love's cousin, for the rest of the day. But now they decided that the weather was too threatening for them to venture outside.

With the trip downtown canceled, Mrs. Love wrote a letter to her husband in Houston.

"The water," she commented, "is pretty—but rough."

While Mrs. Love was writing her letter, Daisy Thorne, the pretty schoolteacher, was taking pictures of the waves from the front porch of her apartment. She saw many persons walking down Broadway, past Lucas Terrace, to get a better view of the spectacle. When Miss Thorne had used all the plates she went inside to work on a pillow cover that she was embroidering for her fiancé's recently opened office in Austin.

From her location near the beach Daisy Thorne had been aware of the overflow before most other Galvestonians. When she awoke that morning she had seen a trickle of water on Broadway, the street that ran in front of Lucas Terrace. It was coming from the giant rollers that were breaking upon the beach, near her building; the end of Broadway had already been covered by the Gulf when Miss Thorne arose that morning. But she, too, felt that this was nothing to worry about; when a child she had gone out in the occasional overflows to splash and play. Even if she had thought there was an occasion for fear, she would have stifled it. Besides, Lucas Terrace was a strong building, and its first floor was raised about two feet above the sand on which it was built.

Lucas Terrace had been erected by an English brick mason who knew his business. He still owned it in 1900. The building's two wings met at right angles. One wing faced east; the other faced south. The Thorne apartment was near the southeast corner of the latter. On the first floor were the kitchen, dining room, storage, and half-bath. Upstairs were the parlor, which faced the Gulf, and immediately behind it, two bedrooms. The rear bedroom was Daisy Thorne's. (On the third floor was another apartment.)

Even as Miss Thorne worked on her embroidery the trickle in Broadway grew to a stream, and before long it covered the avenue; the waves at the end of the avenue were breaking farther inland, flooding more of the area. By eight o'clock Lucas Terrace was surrounded by water, and neighbors from some frail houses in the low areas nearby had come to the building to wait for the water to recede.

4 SATURDAY, 8:00 A.M.–NOON

Raining, Somewhat Blustery

THE TIDE CONTINUED to rise during the remainder of the morning; before long Galvestonians observed that the gutters along most of the streets were filled with water.

These gutters, which offered the only facilities for draining the streets, were from two to three feet deep at the bay and Gulf ends of the city. In the higher parts of the city, however, the depth of the gutters was less—practically nothing at Broadway, which extended generally from west to east along the highest ground in Galveston and acted as a small-scale continental divide.

The water encroaching from both the bay and the Gulf was coming in larger volume from the Gulf side, where the waves were growing ever more tremendous. In the low areas of the city, as the tide continued to rise, water overflowed the gutters and soon those streets were covered. But the higher parts of Galveston were not flooded Saturday morning, and nearly everyone believed that the water would recede before that happened.

The two-mile opening between Bolivar Peninsula and Galveston Island was the only passage that permitted angry Gulf waters to race into Galveston Bay. Between the two jetties extending from the peninsula and the island the torrents of water poured.

40

Anchored or moored in this area—at the east end of Galveston Island—were five vessels. Three English steamships—the *Taunton, Hilarious,* and *Mexican*—were in quarantine; they and the American *City of Everett* were riding at anchor in Bolivar Roads. The government dredge boat *General C. B. Comstock,* then the largest ship of its type in the world, was tied up at a Corps of Engineers coal wharf, built out into the water from the south jetty near the quarantine station. Nearby were other government buildings: inshore from the quarantine station, a Corps of Engineers warehouse, and a Fort San Jacinto torpedo casemate. Several hundred yards distant from this group of buildings were a government lifesaving station and—about 200 yards farther—Fort Point Lighthouse, near the channel entrance.

That morning, while the water was rising in the city's gutters, Captain W. R. Page of the *Taunton* asked his engine room for steam. He wanted it available; by working his engines, he hoped to ease strain on the anchor chain.

Twelve other large steamers were in Galveston, moored along the wharf front on the north side of the city. Among them were the British steamship *Kendal Castle* at Pier 31 (on the west side of the wharf front); the American ship *Alamo* at Pier 24; the Norwegian *Guyller* at 21; the English ships *Benedict, Roma* (commanded by a man named William Storm), and *Norna* at 15; *Comino* at 14; and *Red Cross* at 12 (on the east side of the wharf front).

Shortly after 8:00 A.M. First Mate W. Ledden of the *Comino* made a log entry:

"Saturday, Sept. 8—Commenced with dark, gloomy weather and squalls. Resumed work of putting up shifting boards in 1 and 2 and took on fresh water. The barometer began to fall rapidly and the water to rise."

In the city, while First Mate Ledden was making his log entry, I. H. Kempner was on his way to his office on the second floor of a downtown building.

"It was raining, somewhat blustery," Kempner remembers now, "but nothing to indicate the character of weather we met later in the day."

Kempner had an appointment with Joseph A. Kemp, a Wichita Falls man, and Henry Sayles, a lawyer from Abilene. The three were to discuss awarding a contract for damming a creek just south of Wichita Falls to irrigate several thousand acres of Wichita County land. After Kempner reached the office the weather grew worse.

Many persons now took receivers off the hooks of the wall telephones, rang the operator, and asked for *214*— the number of the Weather Bureau office. The weathermen had only a word of advice for those in the low areas: get to higher ground.

Across town from the Weather Bureau office, on the south side near the beach, five-year-old Sydney Love sailed his toy boat in the flooded streets. Water kept rising, and when it became too deep for youngsters Sydney came inside to his mother.

Another youngster, eight-year-old Sarah Helen Littlejohn, whose father was principal of Broadway School, did not venture from her home at all. With the rain lashing against the windows of her west-side house, she stayed inside and played with a friend, Minnie Lee Borden, who had come over to visit. Minnie Lee was the daughter of L. D. Borden, principal of the Second District School, who lived down the block. The two girls and Sarah's two sisters went upstairs to play dolls.

Across town, the neighbors of Fred Langben were not so calm. (Fred, unmarried, lived in his brother's house on the east side; his brother's wife and four-year-old son had left by train for San Antonio the night before.) From the time Langben's neighbors first felt the north wind and saw the driving rain and the flooded gutters, they were jittery. At intervals they dashed from their house to the corner where the Langben residence stood. They would stop just long enough to look down the street toward the beach, to see how far the water had risen.

On one trip they left the front gate—as well as the door —open. A horse, frightened by the storm, raced north on 12th Street, turned east on Sealy—the street in front of the house—and saw the swinging gate. The animal slowed just enough to go through, went on into the house, and climbed the stairs to the second floor. The horse was to stay there for three days, living on the insides of moss mattresses, until Langben and his manservant roped it and pulled it down rear first. "I've never given a horse the credit a lot of people do," Langben commented later, "but if that one didn't have horse sense no animal ever did."

Several persons who had left their flimsy houses for Lucas Terrace, where they waited for the water to recede, had not had time to eat breakfast. For them Mrs. Thorne cooked biscuits and brewed coffee over her wood stove.

A little more than four miles away from the Thornes, across Bolivar Roads, a few neighbors also had arrived at the well-built residence of H. C. Claiborne, keeper of Port Bolivar Lighthouse.

This lighthouse was at the tip of sparsely settled Bolivar Peninsula, running out from the mainland toward Galveston Island. Near the lighthouse, which was more than 115 feet high, were two houses. One was Claiborne's; the other, the assistant keeper's. Neighbors came there because they were the highest houses in the vicinity.

While families were descending upon their neighbors, the last train to depart from Galveston was leaving Union Passenger Station. It was a Galveston, Houston, and Henderson train, and it was headed for Houston. As it moved over the railroad bridge across the bay, water was creeping up toward the rails.

A short time later, at 9:45 A.M., the last train to enter Galveston was leaving the Houston station fifty miles away. One passenger was A. V. Kellogg, civil engineer in the right-of-way department of the Houston and Texas Central.

"When we crossed the bridge over Galveston Bay the water had risen to within two feet of the level of the track," Kellogg said.

From nine to ten o'clock the showers became such downpours that people working outdoors called a halt and sought shelter.

Henry Ketchum told his men to take the wagons and teams back to the barn, in the rear of his father's house. They had completed transferring the day's shipment of cotton from railroad yards to the compresses anyway.

Pat Joyce, a railroad worker who lived on the extreme west side, was working outside when the rain commenced. His work continued for a while, but it too stopped—a few minutes after nine o'clock.

"I left for home," Joyce said later. (He lived with his widowed sister and her four children, and was their sole support.) "I got there about eleven o'clock and found about three feet of water in the yard. It began to get worse, the water getting higher and the wind getting stronger, until it was almost as bad as the Gulf itself."

At 10:00 A.M., C. A. Paschetag, across the bay on the mainland, also quit work and sought shelter from the rain. He and the men he was with climbed into a nearby Southern Pacific boxcar and closed the door.

But T. C. Bornkessell, a printer in the Weather Bureau office whose job it was to put the forecasts in type and to print them quickly for distribution, went out in the rain. Sometime after 9:00 A.M. he left the office in the Levy Building for his home west of the city. At ten o'clock he passed the residence of E. F. Gerloff, who lived on the west side. Gerloff hailed him to inquire about the weather, and he still remembers Bornkessell's reply that there was no danger. Gerloff is probably the last man to see Bornkessell alive who lived to tell about it.

Shortly after Bornkessell left the Weather Bureau office, another advisory came in by telegraph from the central office in Washington. It was an order to change the northwest storm warning to northeast. Received at 10:10 A.M., Galveston time, it was hoisted five minutes later. (This could put the city in the right semicircle after all.)

By mid-morning, conditions along the wharves were so bad that First Mate Ledden, on the *Comino,* ordered his men to put out extra mooring. He used every inch of line, both wire and Manila, and he dropped the port anchor underfoot. He hoped this would be enough.

At this same time Lucas Terrace was all but cut off from the world. With the exception of a police patrol wagon, which came out a short time later, no vehicle could—or would—make a trip that far east, although some of the worried persons in the building telephoned for hacks.

Conditions were almost as bad on the other side of town. Saint Mary's Orphanage, practically on the beach three miles west of the city, was surrounded by water early in the morning, and by ten o'clock the water was three feet deep. The institution was staffed by ten Sisters of the Incarnate Word; it sheltered ninety-three orphans. One sister, Elizabeth, had gone to market early Saturday morning. When the weather grew threatening, one of the two orphanage workmen had been sent to fetch her. The two still had not returned at ten o'clock.

About ten-thirty Henry Ketchum, having seen that the teams were back in his father's barn, took a horseback ride to the beach. He was able to get to within two blocks of where the beach used to be, and discovered it was not safe to continue. The waves were "breaking over the beach and rolling far inland," he remembers.

While Ketchum was on his jaunt, the *Pensacola*, out in the Gulf, broke her anchor stock. All Friday night the ship had hung on her anchor. Now, with half the morning gone and a storm still blowing, the ship was adrift. Quickly Simmons checked the depth of water. He found his ship was in twenty fathoms. The chart told him that Galveston was northwest about 115 miles. He let out 200 fathoms of nine-inch hawser from the stern. This, with the 100 fathoms of chain on the bow, steadied the ship somewhat.

At 11:00 A.M. Joseph Cline made a special observation to be telegraphed to Washington. The barometer was 29.417, still falling; the temperature was 82.8 degrees, the wind was thirty miles an hour from the north. Nimbus clouds, Cline observed, covered the sky from horizon to horizon, and a heavy rain was falling.

About this time a nurse at John Sealy Hospital, on the east side, found time to start a letter to an out-of-town friend.

"It does not require a great stretch of imagination to imagine this structure a shaky old boat out at sea, the whole thing rocking," she wrote. ". . . Like a reef, surrounded by water . . . water growing closer, ever closer. Have my hands full quieting nervous, hysterical women."

Stuart Godwin, a clerk for a cotton-buying firm, heard at his office downtown that water had crept inland as far as his home on 22nd Street, seven blocks from the beach. He went to a clothing store, bought a bathing suit, and struck out for home, to be near his mother. When he arrived there, the water was above his knees.

By eleven o'clock the Gulf was inland as far as Avenue K in much of the southeastern part of Galveston—almost halfway across the city in some areas. Still most persons were unworried. It was generally true that the longer a person had lived in the island city the less frightened he was by overflows.

Police Chief Ketchum, however, was having a busy day despite the general complacency. He stayed at his desk in the city hall most of the morning, coordinating the work of the department. This consisted largely of answering the telephone and of dispatching the patrol wagon wherever it was required.

The chief was short of help. Early in the morning the day sergeant had been sent home to look after his young son, a victim of what the sergeant feared was lockjaw. At 11:00 A.M. Officer W. H. Plummer, day driver of the patrol wagon, also received permission to go home; water was rising rapidly in the area around his house on the east side. Officer J. T. Rowan took Plummer's place, and a short time later the wagon was sent to Lucas Terrace. A city employee had requested that it be dispatched there to fetch his newly acquired mother-in-law and bring her back to town. (The woman lived in the third-floor apartment above the Thornes.)

When Rowan and his passenger were ready for the return trip, they suggested to Daisy Thorne's mother that she and her family go with them. Mrs. Thorne shrugged this off.

"These people will be hungry," she said of the refugees in her apartment. "Anyway, the building is safe."

The driver clucked at his team, and back to town went the patrol wagon. No more conveyances were to make a trip to Lucas Terrace.

While the patrol wagon was returning to town, a westbound passenger train from Beaumont was chugging along the coast on Bolivar Peninsula, across the channel, nearing the end of another trip. The railroad track ran near Bolivar Lighthouse and continued over the Gulf, on a wood trestle, to deep water. Here the train was to transfer its Galveston-bound passengers to a launch for the final two or three miles of their trip; it arrived at that point shortly before noon every day.

But today the wind was too high and the water was too rough for a launch to take on the passengers. Waves were crashing over the trestle and water was beginning to cover the peninsula itself. After some delay the train started back toward Beaumont, but the water forced the train crew and passengers to seek safety in keeper Claiborne's home near the tall lighthouse. Fortunately for the refugees, Claiborne always bought a month's supply of groceries at a time, and he had just been to market.

In the city, the nurse at Sealy Hospital (in a particularly exposed location, on the city's east side) added another hurried paragraph to her letter while the people from the train walked through the rain into Claiborne's residence:

"Noon: The scenes about here are distressing. Everything washed away. Poor people, trying to save their bedding and clothing. . . . It is a sight. Our beautiful bay a raging torrent."

By noon the Gulf was inland to 12th Street—twelve blocks from the eastern limit of the city—and it gave no indication of receding. On the contrary, it was fast submerging higher land in the city. Tom South, correspondent for the Houston *Daily Post,* reported later that the water was rising about fifteen inches an hour at this time. The pattern for the inundation of higher land was the same as it had been earlier in the morning: towering waves, breaking farther upon the beach, forced water up the street gutters and by noon probably had flooded all of them. The Gulf covered many streets, and still the storm tide sent more water into the heart of the soaked city.

Sarah Littlejohn's oldest sister took time out from playing dolls to go downstairs. When she came up again she said that "papa" was home.

"We all went downstairs and heard papa say that the Pagoda bathhouse was washed away," Sarah wrote a few days later. "Papa said the weather bureau man told him so. It was about 12:00 o'clock then and it was raining hard. The water was not in our yard but was coming in about a block from our house."

Minnie Lee Borden's father came over then and took her home.

At Lucas Terrace, about noon, Daisy Thorne looked out the parlor window across Broadway. The telephone wires were down, and the water was continuing to rise. Miss Thorne proceeded to peer at several cottages on the other side of the street. One of them belonged to John E. Hesse, a cooper at the Mallory Line wharf. Mr. and Mrs. Hesse had three children: Edgar, a grown son who was out of town; Irene, a daughter in her late teens; and Vernon, twelve.

Irene Hesse had become alarmed early in the morning. She left the house and was never seen again. Mr. and Mrs. Hesse and Vernon went to Lucas Terrace after Irene left, without any idea that she had disappeared forever, and they were now in the Thorne apartment.

As Daisy Thorne looked out the window she saw the Hesse cottage collapse, but the Hesses were unaware at the time of their loss.

Many in the apartment did not want to look at the storm at all. Others could not; the space was too crowded for them to get to the window. But Miss Thorne watched everything.

While she watched, Jesse Toothaker, an eighteen-year-old Santa Fe employee, waited for his father in the Union Passenger Station (also the Santa Fe Building) downtown. His father usually came for him at noon to take him home for dinner, but today he failed to appear. Jesse was worried, but there was no telephone in his home, four blocks from the beach, where he lived with his father, mother, and sister. He walked up Strand to the heart of town. Water was rising in the street, and Jesse leaped over frequent pools in his path.

He had not expected to have to buy his dinner, and he had only twenty-five cents. He went into a store and spent ten cents for some licorice candy; then he decided to go back to the Union Passenger Station. He found water so deep on Strand that he detoured to another street for the return trip.

Walter Grover also worked until noon that Saturday. Then, because of the weather, he had dinner at the Elite Restaurant downtown instead of going home.

To this day he remembers that meal. His table was near

the front door. He sat there watching the wind smash panes of glass from the upper stories of nearby buildings.

"The pedestrians on the streets were busy dodging the falling glass," Grover recalls.

After dinner he walked four blocks to the wharf front. There he saw water blown by the north wind submerging the wharves. A schooner was loading flour, although the bay was rough and a drenching rain soaked everything. Later that day the schooner was blown from its pier and was sunk.

Grover went back to the office, but no one was there except a friend, John Adriance, Jr., who worked in a nearby insurance office. He and Adriance went on to Grover's home in the office buggy.

Another friend, Lucian Minor—employed by the same firm for which Grover worked—had left the office before Grover returned. Minor had been conferring with an attorney about a land matter when he received a telephone call from his manservant, Duncan. Water was rising, and Duncan wanted him to take charge of the house, which was almost on the beach. Minor closed his desk and started for his home in the southwest part of the city.

Ephraim Moore, the grocery clerk, always came home for the noon meal; that Saturday he arrived about twelve o'clock. Moore had been making deliveries, and he was only half finished. His wagon was still loaded with groceries, and he had 300 dollars cash in his pocket, collected from morning deliveries.

When Moore drove up to his house he saw that water surrounded it.

"Well," young Jim Moore heard his father say, "it's not going to be anything but high water."

Ephraim Moore wanted to hurry on with his deliveries, but Mrs. Moore refused to let him leave.

"You don't know what's going to happen," she warned.

Moore stayed. He believed that the groceries would be safer in the "basement"—basements in Galveston were nothing more than the walled-in space under the raised first floor—so he took the wagon around to the back, where the door was. Inside the basement was a pile of hay for the animals; the family helped transfer the groceries to the top of the stack.

Dinner was ready, but nobody felt like eating. The water continued to rise.

Attorney Clarence Howth, however, ate his dinner, at Ritter's Saloon and Restaurant downtown. Then he went home in a wagon. He had heard stories of high water in the areas along the beach near his house. Although he supposed they were exaggerated, he decided to investigate.

At Avenue M½, five blocks from his house, the water was several feet deep in the street. Howth left the wagon there and waded to his house, eventually striking water that in some places was up to his shoulders. He climbed the steps to the gallery, stepped out of his shoes, and went inside. Then he greeted his wife and changed into dry clothes.

He made himself comfortable in a chair and lit a cigar. With the unbelievable serenity peculiar to a nineteenth-century Galvestonian who had seen overflows before, he enjoyed a smoke while he watched the fascinating sea.

Some of the small houses near his had already been washed off their foundations, but he was confident of his own. He knew that this overflow was almost over, that the Gulf would "spend itself" before long.

5 SATURDAY, NOON–4:00 P.M.

A Desire for Something
To Cling To

ZACHARY SCOTT, a nineteen-year-old medical student (the
father of actor Zachary Scott), was eager to get up to his
father's ranch near Waco for a last visit with the family
before classes at the University of Texas Medical College
in Galveston reconvened for the new academic year. Medical school, he knew, would not allow time for such activ-
ity.

Late Saturday morning Scott left Saint Mary's Infirmary, where he had been working during the summer as
an orderly, and walked to Union Passenger Station downtown. (Saint Mary's Infirmary, a hospital on the east side,
consisted of a large brick main building; behind it, about
one-fourth of a block away, was a frame building for
Galveston County patients.)

Scott arrived at the passenger depot about 12:15 P.M.

"There was a brisk wind blowing and the tide was
high," Scott recalls. "They told me they weren't selling
any tickets for a while. The tracks across the bay were
being covered by water."

Scott walked back to the infirmary.

By the time he had discovered that the trains were not running, most of the city had ceased trying to do business. Not only were the trains idle; probably no ships except the schooner Walter Grover saw were trying to load cargo, and many employees in business houses had locked up and left for home to help their families.

By this hour some wind gusts had nearly reached storm velocity—a rate of sixty-four to seventy-five miles an hour, according to the Beaufort scale. Around noon it blew at times with the force of a gale. Later it would become a "strong gale," then a "whole gale." Only storm winds and hurricanes are considered stronger. (This scale was devised in 1805 by Admiral Francis Beaufort, an Englishman, for estimating the wind's force. He described a hurricane—Force 12 on his scale—as "that which no canvas could withstand.")

During the morning the wind in Galveston had been mostly from the north, but it had oscillated at intervals between northwest and northeast. It had continued to do so until noon. Now it was mostly from the northeast, and Isaac Cline knew that the wind would come later from the east, southeast, and south. That was the pattern for a tropical hurricane, and the present direction of the wind made it seem certain that Galveston would indeed be in the right semicircle of the storm—the most dangerous— after all. Ships at sea try to avoid at almost any cost being caught in this position.

Cline also feared that when the wind went to the east and southeast it would hurl the Gulf all over Galveston Island. Even with an opposing north wind the Gulf had continued to rise, and now bay water, blown by the north wind, was flooding the north part of town.

On the eastern tip of the island, in Fort Point Lighthouse, Mr. and Mrs. Charles D. Anderson, Sr., had realized their predicament early: they were going to be marooned in the sixty-foot-tall structure, and with their son, Charles D., Jr., up the bay with a surveying party, they would be there alone. But lighthouse keeper Anderson would not have left his station anyway; by early afternoon he could hardly have done so safely, even had he desired.

Anderson, seventy-three, was a West Point graduate, commissioned before the Civil War, and not a timorous man. A native of South Carolina, he resigned his commission—by then a first lieutenancy—April 1, 1861, to join the Confederate army as a captain. He swiftly rose to colonel and commanded the 21st Alabama Infantry Regiment. When Colonel Anderson surrendered Fort Gaines, on an island in Mobile Bay, Admiral David Farragut returned Anderson's sword. The sword now hung in the Andersons' living quarters in Fort Point Lighthouse. On the blade was an inscription: "Returned to Colonel C. D. Anderson by Admiral Farragut for his gallant defense of Fort Gaines, April 8, 1864."

The Andersons lived in quarters—four rooms and a bath —in the upper half of the lighthouse, which was supported by iron piles driven eighteen feet into the sand. The superstructure, topped by a six-sided, glass-enclosed house for the light, was also built of iron. But the living quarters were not as austere as they might have seemed. In fact, the apartment was known to the close friends of its occupants as "Mamma Anderson's dollhouse"; the couple called each other mamma and papa, and the reference was taken from this. Every room reflected Mrs. Anderson's handiwork; each displayed embroidery and fancy laces and other needle work.

The lighthouse was built several yards from the south jetty, on the side away from the channel, and it was linked with the jetty by a narrow steel bridge. Often there was no water around the lighthouse; at high tide there was, at the most, two feet, but the Andersons kept a small boat for possible emergencies.

Early Saturday morning when Anderson had gone outside on a gallery that encircled his living quarters he noticed that the Gulf, agitated by huge swells, had surrounded his lighthouse, and it was much deeper than usual at high tide. By mid-morning the tempestuous water had become several feet deeper and the north wind blew with even greater violence. Now, in the early afternoon, Anderson again walked out onto the gallery, into a pouring rain, to observe the weather. He watched the booming waves breaking over the south jetty, topped by a railroad track that was ordinarily five feet above high tide at this point. He saw that the swells crashing against the lighthouse were drenching a storage platform ten feet below his gallery with salty spray. (On this platform were kept kerosene, fresh water, and wood.)

Anderson's boat was gone, probably smashed into bits; he knew that the steel bridge to the jetty must certainly be carried away if the storm grew worse.

Several hundred yards away from Fort Point Lighthouse three other persons—Dr. John Mayfield, quarantine officer, and his two sons—were virtually marooned at this time inside the quarantine station, an eight-room frame building built above the ground on a small spit extending from the south jetty. It faced Bolivar Roads and the ships anchored there.

Earlier, Dr. Mayfield had sent his wife and two daughters in a yawl to a tug, the *Hygea,* lying off a short dis-

tance. The *Hygea* was to take them to the wharf front in
town and return for the rest of the people at the quarantine station. By the time boatman Henry Sheppard returned in the yawl, Dr. Mayfield had become so concerned
for the safety of two male guests that he put them in the
yawl and told Sheppard to make the south jetty, drop the
men off, and return to the station. He believed that the
men could make their way down the jetty, although waves
were at times crashing over it, to the coal wharf and the
government dredge *Comstock,* still tied up there. Mayfield attempted to send his two sons too, but they refused
to leave him.

In the rough water, however, Sheppard could not make
a landing at the jetty. He jumped out in chest-deep water
and was going to try to guide the yawl back to the quarantine station. But Mayfield signaled him to go on into
town; pushing a boat in this water was dangerous, if not
absolutely impossible. After a slow trip through seas that
frequently seemed about to swamp the boat, Sheppard
and his passengers arrived safely at Pier 16.

Had Sheppard been able to make the south jetty, his
passengers probably could not have reached the *Comstock*
anyway. John Hanson, a longshoreman who lived near
the quarantine station, had been trying to get to the *Comstock,* after his house collapsed, at exactly the same time.
Hanson observed the waves breaking over the jetty, and
it seemed to him unlikely that he would ever be able to
get all the way to the coal wharf. He was debating where
to go for refuge when he saw the yawl in trouble, and he
had started to help Sheppard with the boat when Sheppard was signaled into town. Hanson then had made his
way to the Corps of Engineers warehouse, behind the
quarantine station. Later, when that fell, he struggled

through the water to the nearby torpedo casemate—a large masonry structure covered with sand, so that it formed a giant mound—climbed on top of it, and burrowed into the sand.

By the time Hanson had taken refuge in the warehouse, the *Hygea* had returned for Dr. Mayfield and his sons. But Mayfield now had no yawl for a trip out to the tug, and she had no boat to send for him. Mayfield signaled the captain to go back to town, and the quarantine officer and his two sons were isolated in the station.

Although the Fort Point area, unprotected as it was at the eastern end of the island, felt the brunt of the storm earlier than other areas, the first death of the day probably occurred in the city. About 1:00 P.M. a baby fell out a window of a house on 21st Street near Avenue N and drowned in water that covered the yard. However, nobody ever was able to say for certain that this was the storm's first victim.

At that same time the last train to get into Galveston was creeping toward Union Passenger Station. This was the train that had left Houston at 9:45 A.M.

If the passengers were unlucky to get there in time for the hurricane, they were indeed fortunate to arrive at all. Passenger A. V. Kellogg later related how the train, after crossing the bay bridge and reaching a point two miles beyond, was stopped by a washout. An hour passed before a relief train was able to come out on the nearby Galveston, Houston, and Henderson track. In that time, Kellogg said, the water rose a foot and a half and covered all of the rails.

When the relief train arrived in the vicinity, it signaled the nine-forty-five from Houston to back up half a mile, where the ground was slightly higher. There Kellogg and the other passengers were transferred. The G. H. & H. crew had to wade ahead of the relief train engine and dislodge debris from the track on the trip to town.

Fifteen minutes later railroad officials attempted to ignore the elements and schedule a train out of Galveston. The train could not even get out of the yards before water forced it to return.

By this time—shortly before 2:00 P.M.—the Andersons, in Fort Point Lighthouse, were completely cut off from the rest of the world; the bridge from the lighthouse to the jetty had collapsed, as Anderson had foreseen.

Captain Edward Haines, in charge of the government lifesaving station about 200 yards from the lighthouse, realized that the couple were trapped. He ordered his men into a boat and made for the lighthouse.

It was hopeless. The sea tossed Haines and his men about so violently that they could make little headway, and Haines brought his boat back to the station. Two hours after Haines returned, the station collapsed; Mrs. Haines and one of the men were drowned.

"It was a noble act for Captain Haines to attempt to rescue us," Mrs. Anderson said later, "but it was a useless risk. Papa wouldn't have left the lighthouse while it stood, and I would never have left without him."

At this hour the Reverend Judson B. Palmer, Y.M.C.A. secretary, was sitting at a desk in his office on the third floor of the Y.M.C.A. building, near the central part of town. A neighbor telephoned to tell Palmer that his wife wanted him to come home. Water, the neighbor said, was getting deep in the vicinity of the Palmer residence four blocks from the beach, and the Palmers' telephone was out.

The reverend rode a wagon to within half a block of his house, and he waded from there.

"Mrs. Palmer was anxious and thought we ought to go to the Y.M.C.A. building," Palmer said later. "I told her she and Lee [their young son] could go and I would stay and look after things, but she wouldn't go then."

After Lucian Minor had left Trueheart's, where he and Walter Grover worked, he had hurried toward home, walking west on Broadway to 35th Street, a raised shell road that made for easier footing. At Avenue S, three blocks from the beach, he turned westward again; only then did he realize the danger of being outside. He could hardly make his way through the water.

"Lucian had less reason than most men to anticipate any danger from being out in the storm," his brother Farrell observed later. "In the storm of 1867 he and a friend stayed in the sand hills—near Lucian's house—in perfect safety while they watched a coal-laden vessel being driven ashore. In the storm of 1875 he and I, with thousands of others, walked everywhere."

This one, however, was worse than the others. Yet Lucian Minor felt he had to go on. He had not told Duncan to go to a safer place, and he was sure the servant would still be at home waiting for him.

With great difficulty he struggled through the water for eight more blocks, and he was still twenty blocks from home. Getting there, he concluded, was impossible. He knocked at the door of William Miller, manager of a downtown market, who lived near the corner of Avenue S and 43rd Street.

Miller's house was a sturdy one. Several other persons were in it when Minor arrived. One of these was Patrick

Joyce, who had quit work during the morning because of the rain. His sister and her four children were there also.

Some sixteen blocks farther west from the place in which Lucian Minor had sought refuge, eight members of the Wiley T. Allen family were leaving their house for a stronger one nearby. In this family were Mr. and Mrs. Allen, Bill and Herbert (twins), Lucy, and Claude, and Ralph and Florence Klaes. The latter two were brother and sister who had been living with the Allens since 1895 as adopted children.

Saturday had not turned out at all as the Allens had expected. For several days they had been looking forward to going down the island to a housewarming, and in 1900 that meant a gay time: a big crowd, a table of food, and dancing until the early hours of the morning. Bill and Herbert with great reluctance had given up the hope of going to the party; despite the rain, which by the middle of the morning had become a deluge, the two youths had put on their suit trousers and starched white shirts with standing collars. Bill, the taller of the two, was a six-footer, and he seemed even taller when dressed in his Sunday best.

Shortly after the twins had finished dressing, Allen had seen the yard full of water. He went out in the rain and tasted it.

"Anna," he told his wife, "that's salt water. We're having an overflow."

Now, about 2:00 P.M., the Allens had decided to leave their home for a nearby house that seemed safer. In it lived Bill Letts, who was captain of a red-snapper schooner, his wife, and two children. Letts' sister-in-law and her child were visiting them.

Bill Allen carried his eighty-six-year-old grandmother

pickaback to the Letts' house. Then he returned for a seventy-year-old neighbor—Mrs. Martha McMillan—Mrs. McMillan's granddaughter, and Florence Klaes, and carried them over to the house. He was still wearing his dress clothes, and they were thoroughly soaked.

By two o'clock that afternoon I. H. Kempner was extremely worried about conditions at home. He and the two men, Kemp and Sayles, who had been conferring about the dam for the irrigation project in Wichita County, were still in Kempner's office.

Kemp and Sayles decided to go to Union Passenger Station and take a train out. There the ticket agent told them the same thing he had told Zachary Scott earlier. Kempner took a horse and buggy home, where he found several neighbors gathered to wait out the storm.

Four blocks from the beach, S. O. Young waded through water to reach his house. He was glad that he had sent his wife a telegram early that morning advising her to stay in San Antonio with the children. When Young reached home he saw that water was a foot deep on his lot, although the sidewalk in front of the house had been curbed up about four feet and his whole lot had been raised four to five feet above the street level.

About two miles southwestward down the beach from Young was Fort Crockett, and the water there was as deep as it was around Young's residence. At Fort Crockett, located in an area known as the Denver Resurvey, were a heavy battery of ten-inch guns, a battery of eight ten-inch mortars, and a rapid-fire battery. Manning those guns were Battery O soldiers of the First Artillery, under Captain W. C. Rafferty. Another part of Battery O was at

Fort San Jacinto, on Fort Point, where the Army had its most important fortifications.

At two o'clock Captain Rafferty and a detail of men were examining one of the ten-inch guns when Rafferty became alarmed by the high water. He sent one man back to his quarters to bring Mrs. Rafferty, the children, and a servant to the gun. The captain believed that a small steel room beneath the gun carriage would make a good shelter.

He watched the man make his way through the water. Within five minutes he was horrified to see the soldier swept off his feet and drowned. Rafferty quickly stripped off his shirt and trousers and, half swimming, half wading, reached his quarters. He advised the men in the wood barracks nearby to get out. Then he put his children on an improvised raft, their backs to the spray. He and his wife guided the raft to the gun.

The steel room was without ventilation; the Gulf pounded the gun and broke over it, but the Rafferty family was safe.

When the captain's message to evacuate the barracks came, the men of Battery O were divided in sentiment. Some wanted to stay rather than venture out in this weather, but the first sergeant told his men he was leaving.

"This building won't stand half an hour," he said. "It's every man for himself."

Of the more than forty artillerymen in the barracks, the sergeant and some thirty others struck out for Denver Resurvey School several blocks away. Three were drowned on the way.

Shortly before the artillerymen left for the school building, Walter Grover arrived home in the office buggy.

"When I got there my sister Mable, who was visiting us, wanted to see the storm. So did I. Although we could hardly stand against the wind, and the water was axle deep, we drove as far as Eleventh and Winnie. By then water was in the buggy, so I told her we must go back. But she wanted to go on toward the beach.

"I told her that it was likely that the boards over the gutters would float away and the horse would step into a gutter and maybe break a leg. Then we would have to swim home."

They went back. Grover let his sister out at home and Grover and Adriance took the horse and buggy to a stable in the back of the Adriance home several blocks away. But Grover wanted to see more of the storm himself; so the two young men set out on foot.

By 2:30 P.M. Jess Simpson and his brother Bill, who comprised the crew of a two-masted, ninety-four-foot-long schooner called the *Hard Times,* had become so fearful of the weather and the increasingly high winds that they cast off from Pier 19 and set sail for the mouth of the San Jacinto River, northward up the bay, where the vessel would be safer.

Jess, the captain, was 25 years old. He had lost one eye in the Spanish-American War. Bill, five years younger, was the mate. The two brothers had been engaged in hauling hand-hewn railroad ties and cord wood to Galveston from a point about ten miles up the San Jacinto; they had unloaded their most recent cargo two days before the storm.

"When we got out of the harbor we could see the open bay, and it looked so rough that we decided not to try it," Bill Simpson remembers now. "We sailed to a position just north of Pelican Island and let go our big anchor, which weighed 300 pounds. Then we dropped two other anchors."

The two thought they would be in a protected place, with Galveston and Pelican islands between their vessel and the Gulf.

"The water was not very rough at that time where we were," Bill Simpson recalls, "but the wind was terrific."

About the same time the Simpsons were leaving Pier 19 in the *Hard Times*, Joseph Cline was going to the roof of the Levy Building for a 2:30 P.M. reading. He discovered that the rain gauge had blown away. The last reading was 1.27 inches, but the Weather Bureau office later estimated that a total of about ten inches of rain fell. (This guess was based on the records of nearby stations.)

Cline also noted a barometer reading of 29.166, a temperature of 82.8, a wind of forty-two miles an hour from the northeast. Nimbus clouds coming from the northeast still covered the sky, he observed, and a heavy rain continued to fall. (The wind velocity was somewhat misleading. The Weather Bureau took as its official reading the velocity over a five-minute period. Actually there were gusts stronger than forty-two.)

The Weather Bureau office was now besieged with telephone calls. Cline and John Blagden, a meteorologist from the Memphis station on temporary duty at Galveston, spent much of their time advising frantic callers to get to the highest ground, for the worst was still to come. But a great many Galvestonians never had the advantage of receiving this or any previous warning. Many telephones were already out of order; and in 1900 telephones were a luxury that relatively few could afford.

Joseph Cline had just completed the special observation to be sent to Washington when Isaac Cline, still on the south side of town warning people to leave, took time out long enough to telephone the office. He realized, by this time, that "an awful disaster" was upon the city.

"The Gulf is rising rapidly," he told his brother. "Half the city is under water."

He then relayed some additional information to send the chief of the Weather Bureau in Washington.

"I stated that the city was fast going under water, and that great loss of life must result," Isaac Cline said. "I stressed the need for relief."

Joseph Cline added to his report the information his brother gave him and left for the Western Union Telegraph office about two blocks from the Levy Building. The pavement of wood blocks throughout the business section was afloat and up to the level of the raised sidewalks. He waded through churning water, knee deep in places, breaking through the floating pavement with each step. After finally reaching the Western Union office, he learned that for two hours the wires had been down.

Joseph Cline then struck out for the Postal Telegraph office, a few doors beyond Western Union. Their wires too, he learned, had been down two hours. He made his way back through the floating blocks to the Weather Bureau office.

A last chance remained. He picked up the telephone and asked for a long-distance connection with the Western Union office in Houston.

"Sorry," he was told; there were several thousand calls waiting ahead of him. He pleaded that his was a vital government message, but to no avail. Then he asked for the manager, Tom Powell. Fortunately Powell was there, and Joseph Cline explained his problem. The manager gave him a connection to Houston. Cline filed the message, requesting officials at the telegraph office to treat it as confidential. ("Galveston and Houston were traditional rivals," Cline later explained.)

Some time after 3:00 P.M., at almost the very instant Joseph Cline finished sending his message, the long-distance wire snapped. Galveston now was isolated from the world. Cline's message describing the city's plight was the last one to be sent until after the storm.

Mrs. Frank Walker had been invited to a birthday party Saturday afternoon for Mrs. Henry Cortes, Sr., who lived in the central section of the city, and she was not to be deterred by the weather. Her sister, Mrs. Corinne Loftus, had arrived from Houston in the morning, and the two ate dinner early so they would not arrive late at the party. While Joseph Cline was returning from the Postal Telegraph office, Mrs. Loftus was going to the Cortes home. C. J. Michaelis, son-in-law of Mrs. Cortes, had come in his horse and buggy about three o'clock to pick them up, but there was room for just one passenger at a time.

"Corinne wrapped up and went first," Mrs. Walker wrote her mother two days later. "The water was about three feet deep then, and the wind was getting stronger all the time."

For some time Mrs. Walker had been worried about the water rising in the yard. Before Michaelis had come for her sister, she had called her husband at Clarke and Courts, told him she was going to the Cortes residence, and suggested that he come home to look after the horse. Walker understood his wife to say that she was going to the Courts' residence; George M. Courts, president of

Clarke and Courts, lived about four blocks from the Walkers.

When Michaelis returned for Mrs. Walker her husband still had not arrived, but she put on his high-topped rubber boots and prepared to leave. As an afterthought she picked up a few pieces of jewelry and her husband's purse. When she stepped into the yard water poured into the boots.

"Neither Corinne nor I had a hat on; we put blankets over our heads," Mrs. Walker remembers. "I wore the oldest clothes I had."

While his wife was leaving the house, Walker was making his way home, but his progress through the water was slow. It was so deep in places that he had to swim. On the way he met a neighbor, Alexander Coddou. Coddou's wife was out of the city, and he was going home to look after their five children. No one ever saw Coddou or the children alive after that.

When Walker reached home he hitched Bess to the buggy and drove through the water to the residence of George Courts. His wife and sister-in-law were not there. He realized she must have said "Cortes" and left for that house.

At three o'clock water was three feet above the wharf, and "all manner of wreckage" was lashing the *Comino,* First Mate Ledden wrote in the log.

At the same hour the family of Edwin J. Pettibone fled their small, raised cottage in the southwestern part of the city for the safety of a large two-story house nearby, belonging to John Wood Harris. Pettibone, a mounted policeman, had with him his wife, who was Walter Grover's sister Louisa, and their youngest son, Earl.

When the Pettibones entered the residence, a strong house built of Southern yellow pine, Rebecca Harris, Mrs. Pettibone's close friend for many years, met them at the door.

"Lulu," Miss Harris said to Mrs. Pettibone, "don't stay downstairs where all kinds of people are coming in. Go up to my room."

The Pettibones went upstairs. They had just reached Miss Harris' room when they felt the house settling. The ceiling fell in, but the rafters caught on the window sills and prevented it from going all the way to the floor and crushing the Pettibones. They found themselves trapped in a triangular space between the floor, side wall, and ceiling, and the rest of the house seemed ready to collapse at any moment.

Earl squirmed through an opening in the ceiling, where the chimney had been, onto the roof. His parents followed. They held a lightning rod to keep from being blown off by a wind which later ripped Mrs. Pettibone's clothes to shreds. The rain stung them unmercifully, but they stayed there. (Sunday morning they found their own small home relatively undamaged.)

At about the same time the Pettibones were leaving their residence, Mrs. Love's mother saw Henry Locke, a seaman who lived across the street, leaving his house. He was in the water pushing a boat; his wife was in it. Mrs. Love's mother called him to her house and asked if the weather was going to get worse.

No, he said, it should get better about five o'clock when the tide changed.

Nevertheless, she asked the man if he would take Mrs. Love, Sydney, and May Mitchell, another guest in the house, to Saint Mary's University six blocks away.

Locke would. Mrs. Love took with her a prayer book containing her return ticket to Houston, a handkerchief that she was embroidering, and a box of valuables she had brought to Galveston. There were no good-bys; but Mrs. Love never saw her mother and grandmother again.

Surprisingly, Locke encountered no great difficulty in reaching Saint Mary's University. He left Mrs. Love, Sydney, and May Mitchell with several other refugees in a one-story frame clubhouse on the university grounds; then Locke and his wife went on to the home of a relative.

Rising water soon forced those in the clubhouse to seek the safety of the main building half a block away. Several men in the crowd helped the women across. Two men, one on each side, escorted May Mitchell; then they returned to assist another woman to the main building. One man carried Sydney Love on his shoulders.

Mrs. Love was last to be escorted from the clubhouse. As she and the two men neared the main building, she was blown from their grasp and thrown under water. The men grabbed her quickly, but she became hysterical; she remembers very little about what happened after that.

Her young son, however, was unmoved by all the excitement. He still remembers that when he was taken to the second floor of the building the first thing his wondering eyes saw was a cow.

"I've often wondered how they got that cow down from there," Sydney Love says today. (He never has found out. But the morning after the storm he was one of the few youngsters in Galveston lucky enough to have fresh milk for breakfast.)

At three o'clock the Sealy Hospital nurse, who had started writing a running commentary on the storm that

morning, hurriedly penned another paragraph of her letter to the out-of-town friend:

"Am beginning to feel a weakening desire for something to cling to. Should feel more comfortable in the em-
brace of your arms. You hold yourself ready to come to
us should the occasion demand?"

Now the storm felled the residence of *News* telegraph
editor R. B. Spangler and the barracks where twelve of
the Battery O men had chosen to stay.

Spangler's family had left about one o'clock; he had
stayed with the house, anxiously looking out the south
windows most of the time, until the house moved over
slowly and settled in the water. Spangler rushed out and
made his way through the storm to the house where his
family had fled.

Of the twelve men left in the barracks when it fell in on
them, seven were swept away. The others survived by
grabbing wreckage and clinging to it for the next few
hours.

After Walter Grover and John Adriance left their horse
and buggy in the stable they walked west on Avenue K
to 23rd Street.

"John had on a new yellow slicker that caught both the
wind and water," Grover recalls. "It hampered his leg
movements. When we reached Twenty-third and L, John
was exhausted. He turned back, but I continued out
Twenty-third. When I reached O-and-a-half the water
was so deep I decided it was time for me to get back
home too."

Grover made his way back on the east side of 23rd
Street, where he was somewhat sheltered from the wind
and where the westward rush of the water was not so

fierce. But he was lucky to get home. He saw several persons struck down and probably killed by flying slate from house roofs. Two others drowned before his eyes when they were carried under water by debris. The wreckage, Grover remembers with awe, was carried down the street "faster than a man could have run on dry ground." A man making his way through the storm had very little chance when a mass of debris was blown his way.

While Grover struggled homeward, seventeen-year-old Walter Bergstrom, who worked in a downtown bicycle shop, was watching the effects of the storm with great interest. He stood in the vicinity of the wharves near the bicycle shop, curiously following the efforts of ships' crews to keep their vessels alongside the piers. By now all the ships probably had every available inch of line out to the wharves.

Shortly before 4:00 P.M. Walter returned to the bicycle shop and observed that the water had risen swiftly. He hung his own bicycle on hooks high up the wall, and he remembers now how the others laughed at him. Water, they thought, would never get that deep. (Six months later young Bergstrom was the only one of the group who had a bicycle left. Salt water had seeped into the hollow parts of the metal frames of the other bicycles, and it had rusted them from the inside out. Months later, pedaling down the street, the owner would find his means of transportation going to pieces beneath him.)

After hanging his bicycle, Walter waded more than a mile home.

Some time between 3:00 P.M. and 4:00 P.M. the bay met the Gulf, and the waters joined in a bacchanalian dance through the streets. The exact time that this occurred is not known for certain, but by four o'clock water was a foot deep even at the highest point in the city, and the wind had reached hurricane velocity. Soon the rest of the island went under, including the fifteen-foot-high area in its middle. From the air Galveston Island would have greatly resembled a submarine about to surface, if one could have seen it through the storm.

Several survivors remember seeing wreckage being swept toward the Gulf at this time, and they thought that at last the water had begun to recede; it was carrying wreckage back with it as it fell, they reasoned. Later they were to realize what was actually happening: the entire city was submerged, and bay water and the northeasterly wind had swept the wreckage they saw completely across the city.

Four blocks from the beach, the Gulf was on S. O. Young's first floor. When he arrived home, some time after two o'clock, he had calmly observed the storm, as Clarence Howth had done earlier.

"I sat on the front gallery and watched the water," Young said. "It rose gradually until the third step was under water. Then it apparently stopped rising and was stationary. My large two-story frame house stood on brick pillars about four feet high, and I had no fear of water coming in it."

Now, at four o'clock, water was on the first floor and still rising. Young already had secured the doors and windows as best he could and moved up to the second floor. There was nothing to do but watch the storm. This he did from a chair near a window overlooking Avenue P½. He saw that water was racing westward down that street.

About one block from Young's house was the residence of Y.M.C.A. secretary Palmer. At four o'clock Palmer saw

Isaac Cline pass in front of his house on the way home to his family. Palmer later remembered, "I called to him, and he said to stay in the house, as it was strong."

Neighbors knew Palmer's house was well built and began abandoning their homes for the safety afforded by his residence. Eventually there were seventeen persons there.

Far up the bay at Morgan's Point, the water had continued to rise, as it did in Galveston. Henry Henke, whose name now appears on Henke and Pillot supermarkets throughout South Texas, sent his driver with the carriage to pick up his friends, the Curtins. With her husband away in Houston, Mrs. Curtin did not want to leave the house, and Henke's driver returned without her. But Annie Campbell, the Curtins' maid, went with him.

In Galveston, Police Chief Ketchum, responding to a call, ordered the patrol wagon to Sixth Street and Winnie Avenue to evacuate a family. Rowan was accompanied on this trip by Officer J. C. Byrd. The two policemen found that they could not reach their destination in the wagon, and requisitioned a nearby boat. Then they ran across Plummer, the regular day driver of the wagon who had been given permission to go home that morning, and the three officers evacuated 100 persons from the block. Ketchum and only one man, Officer E. M. Johnson, had been left at headquarters, and Rowan and Byrd returned as quickly as they could.

Although Sixth and Winnie was only three blocks from Lucas Terrace, it would have been impossible for the policemen to get there even if they had tried.

Miss Thorne and her mother were with the others on the second floor of the apartment in Lucas Terrace now, and the young teacher was quickly losing her indifference toward the seriousness of this overflow.

Mrs. Thorne had stayed downstairs in the kitchen for a while, although water had covered the floor ankle deep. Sloshing around, she had tended her wood stove and prepared biscuits and coffee for the latest arrivals. Then she went upstairs. Daisy Thorne went downstairs after that to open the first-floor doors, easing the pressure, and the Gulf splashed into the Thorne apartment uncontested. Miss Thorne then carried five cats from the first floor to the parlor. She made three trips before getting them all upstairs; by then the water was knee deep on the first floor.

All day long Miss Thorne had persisted in her belief that this storm would blow over, as had all the others. But now she questioned her belief. At four o'clock there were no other houses left standing in the neighborhood of Lucas Terrace; and the howling wind gave no indication that it was going to subside. The water around the apartment building was rising to a height that Miss Thorne could never have imagined.

6 SATURDAY, 4:00–6:00 P.M.

Caught in a Trap

BY FOUR O'CLOCK thirteen-year-old Jim Moore and a brother and sister were being pushed in a bathtub toward Unger's grocery, a block away from their home. Jim's father and mother, with a neighbor's help, guided the tub. After proceeding about half a block they reached a comparatively shallow section, and Jim was able to get out and walk.

The Moores had never eaten their dinner, and the table was still set when they abandoned their home. After helping Ephraim Moore unload the groceries, the family had thought of little else except the weather. With the water still rising in the early afternoon, they had brought the groceries from on top of the hay in the basement to the first floor. Then they had taken about 100 frightened chickens, one by one, from roosts in the flooded coop in the back yard to the safety of a second-floor bedroom.

"What'll I do with the dog?" Jim Moore had asked his father after the chickens had been carried upstairs.

"Put him in with the chickens!"

After Moore had seen the groceries and chickens safely into the house, he came inside, took off his vest, and hung the garment on a chair. He put the 300 dollars collected

76

for groceries in a bag in the dresser drawer. (Moore never saw the money again.) Then a neighbor came over through the water and asked Moore to help him move his family out of the house.

Moore obliged. He helped the neighbor rip out a copper lined wood bathtub and helped guide the tub, the family in it, through the water to a safer house. After the neighbor's family had gone inside, Moore asked the man to help him evacuate his own family. But the neighbor refused.

"If you don't come help me," Moore told him, "you'll never live to join your family inside that house."

The man pondered the matter for a moment. Finally he chose to help push the tub carrying Moore's three children to Unger's grocery.

Unger's was packed when they arrived. People from several blocks around had gathered there to wait out the storm. At least one soldier from Fort Crockett, about fourteen blocks away, had sought refuge there.

Jim's brother, Walton, had worn his bathing suit over to the grocery store, and now the girls in the crowd were teasing him about it. Walton was abashed, so he slipped out, hoping his parents would not notice, went back home, put on his clothes, and made his way back to Unger's.

Meanwhile, Walter P. Fisher, prescription clerk at a downtown drugstore, was leaving the store to see about his family. Fisher was only halfway home when some men inside a house saw him staggering along the street. Hurriedly, they rescued him from the water. Fisher was near a state of collapse, but after resting inside the house for a few minutes, he insisted on continuing.

"If anything happens to me," he said before he departed, "tell my wife I tried to reach her."

He died in the storm, after going only a short distance. Probably he would have been unable to reach his house anyway; it was so near the beach that, at the height of the storm, it collapsed. Fisher's wife and three children all lost their lives.

Shortly after 4:00 P.M. the people in George Boschke's house, where Mrs. Vidor, King, and the two boys from Fort Worth had sought shelter from the rain that morning, concluded that they had better flee to higher ground. Boschke's house was not raised as high as most others in the neighborhood, and water had covered the first floor.

When Mrs. Vidor had left the beach that morning she had intended only to deliver the two Fort Worth boys to their parents, who were visiting the Boschkes. Planning to return, with King, to her own house after the rain stopped, she had telephoned her husband immediately and told him where she was.

"Stay where you are," Vidor instructed, "and I'll come get you."

The Boschkes, close friends of the Vidors, then insisted that the Vidors stay for dinner. When her husband failed to arrive in time for the meal, Mrs. Vidor tried to call him again. She found that the telephone connection was broken.

Mr. and Mrs. Boschke and their guests finally seated themselves at the table. As they ate they saw water trickling into the house under the doors; the men in the group quickly left the table and began rolling up the rugs.

After that nobody felt any desire to finish the meal. When the water continued to rise, they decided that the

Kenison residence, two blocks up the street, seemed a safer haven; they struck out for it.

Mrs. Vidor stepped off the front gallery into waist-deep water, and the hurricane winds almost blew her off her feet.

"We'll never make it," Boschke shouted, and everyone went back into the house.

Boschke was aware of what would happen next. He said, "Throw open all the doors and windows, and let the water anchor the house." Then he suggested they take the food from the dinner table to the second floor. That done, they seated themselves on the stairway in the center of the Boschkes' large hall and watched the water rise in the house. As it crept up, they moved, one step at a time, toward the second floor.

Fifteen blocks northeast of the Boschke residence, the water around the home of the Charles P. McNeills, who were out of town, was not yet so deep, but it was deep enough to cause the McNeills' servant some concern for the safety of McNeill's thoroughbred horses. He improvised a ramp and led the horses from their stable to a first-floor rear room. There he used a charcoal brazier to dry the animals. The mark left by the brazier on the floor was there more than half a century later.

At 4:30 P.M. Lieutenant H. P. McIntosh, U.S.N., left the branch hydrographic office in the Levy Building, which had begun to rock "in a most unpleasant manner." With difficulty he made his way through the water and flying debris to the Tremont Hotel, two blocks away.

The lobby of the Tremont was packed. Nearly 700 persons hovered there while the wind acted as a battering ram against the walls of the building. They reacted with a mixture of wails and prayers to the announcements made every few minutes about the height of the water outside.

The crowd grew as more and more bedraggled refugees struggled through water and hurricane winds to the safety of the hotel. Some, losing their footing in deep water, never made it; they were carried under and drowned. Others were struck by flying slate and timber.

The hotel lobby was a dry and relatively comfortable shelter, although the roar of the wind was anything but pleasant. A few guests tried passing the time by dancing, laughing, and joking—but not for long.

Shortly before five o'clock the Gulf came into the Tremont lobby, slithering under the door like a snake and spreading out immediately once the entrance was gained. Now an increasingly hysterical crowd, which grew to include close to 1000 at the height of the storm, hurried up the stairs to the mezzanine.

At 5:15 P.M., just forty-five minutes after McIntosh left the Levy Building for the Tremont, the Weather Bureau's wind gauge atop the building blew away. Galveston never knew the force of the wind that battered it after that. The last recorded velocity was eighty-four miles an hour for the five-minute period the Weather Bureau accepted as official. For two of those minutes, however, the wind registered close to 100 miles an hour. The weathermen estimated a velocity of "110 or 120 miles an hour" after that, and some guesses go even higher.

Six blocks away from the Levy Building, Morris Sheppard was marooned in Union Passenger Station. He had gone there with W. A. Fraser about mid-afternoon to catch a train out of the city, but by that time it was much too late.

A few days after the storm Sheppard recalled the experience: "The weather got so bad we decided to leave. We went to the Union Station to catch a train that was to leave for Houston. When the storm broke everybody went upstairs."

There, packed in a room with 100 others, Sheppard was to pass some of the most terrifying hours of his life. In the same room were Toothaker, the young man who had bought the licorice at noon, and Kemp and Sayles, who had been talking about the irrigation project with I. H. Kempner.

Also huddled in a room, but on the east side of town a mile and a half away, were the people in the Thornes' apartment. Everyone was in the parlor now, on the second floor, and they were terrified by the sound of furniture bobbing on top of the water, bumping against the very floor on which they stood. For Daisy Thorne this was the first moment of real fear. It was to become even more intense within the next few minutes.

Next to the Thorne apartment was flat Number 4, in the southeast corner of the building. Part of it was in the east wing and part in the south, with entrances facing each of those two directions. There were two apartments in the flat; one occupied the first and second floors, the other occupied the third. In the lower apartment were gathered several frightened women and one man—J. P. McCauley, husband of the woman who had been painting Daisy Thorne as a woodland nymph. McCauley was a paralytic.

The group in flat Number 4 heard a section of the lower wall collapse beneath them, and they knew then that they had to leave or face certain death in a hail of bricks and concrete when the upper wall fell too. But leaving was not so simple; each flat in Lucas Terrace was a separate unit, and there were no doors connecting one with another.

The group moved up to the third floor. They found an ironing board and placed it across the space between the galleries of this apartment and the one above the Thornes'. Unprotected from the wind, and with the water slapping against the building just below their precarious walk, the women—carrying McCauley—somehow made it across the ironing board into the third-floor apartment of flat Number 5. Then they went downstairs into the Thorne apartment.

When the crowd that was huddled there learned that part of the wall next door had collapsed, they realized with horror their predicament. It would be only a question of time before the rest of the building collapsed.

Mrs. Thorne took out the family Bible.

"The Lord is my shepherd; I shall not want," she read aloud. ". . . Yea, though I walk through the valley of the shadow of death, I will fear no evil; for thou art with me."

The thumping of the furniture against the ceiling below accompanied her words. When she finished reading, most of the people prayed. As they did so, waves dashed over the tops of the windows of the room they were in, shutting out most of what little daylight remained.

At 5:00 P.M. they heard the rest of flat Number 4 fall. Moving somewhere else was a necessity, but every move seemed hopeless.

They went into Mrs. Thorne's bedroom, just back of the parlor. McCauley, who had been put on Mrs. Thorne's bed, was already there. His wife was sitting beside him. Someone suggested going up to the third floor, to get as far as possible from the water. Someone else proposed going on to the rear bedroom—Daisy Thorne's—on the side of the building away from the Gulf. Eventually they agreed that the latter plan was the wiser, and twenty-two persons packed themselves into the tiny room. But the McCauleys stayed in Mrs. Thorne's bedroom; McCauley had found the big bed comfortable, and his wife refused to leave him.

A hall collapsed just as the last person squeezed into Daisy Thorne's bedroom. Flying bricks knocked out a window of the room, and debris came hurtling in. Miss Thorne ran into her mother's bedroom to get pillows to shield her mother and aunt. She grabbed the pillows and paused long enough to offer to help Mrs. McCauley carry her husband into the rear room, but still the McCauleys chose to stay where they were. Before she got back into her room the parlor fell, and Daisy Thorne had an unobstructed view of the Gulf.

The rest of Lucas Terrace might have had a chance had it not been for some big timbers from the government construction on Fort Point. They had been carried westward by the current, crushing everything in their path. What was left of the east wing withstood the timbers at first, but each succeeding crash weakened the structure. Finally it collapsed.

Miss Thorne heard the roar. She glanced through the broken window of her room to see the wing fall "like a house of cards." Then Mrs. Thorne's bedroom fell, with the McCauleys still in it.

In all earnestness Daisy Thorne prepared to meet her death.

After Joseph Cline had sent the last message out of Galveston, he left the office in the care of John Blagden, who stayed there during the rest of the storm. Cline struck out for the beach area, hoping he could help his brother warn people, even now, to flee to the center of town. He also wanted to be near his brother's house; its inhabitants might need help.

Joseph Cline waded through flooded streets, gusts of wind blowing him completely off his path. Along the way he shouted warnings that the worst part of the storm was yet to come. When people could not hear him over the wind, he pointed to the center of the city, urging them to go in that direction.

Still many residents stayed in their homes. Some were confident that their sturdily constructed houses could weather the storm. But they also realized that venturing out into the storm had become too dangerous to attempt. Slate sharp enough to decapitate a person was flying through the air, carried by a wind approaching 100 miles an hour. As if that hazard were not enough, there were also bricks and pieces of wood that could kill a man if they hit him in the right spot. And hitting him anywhere could mean broken bones and perhaps helpless drowning after that.

Ironically, the slate roofs had been required by city ordinance after a disastrous fire ravaged Galveston in 1885. One of the few buildings that had not burned in the razed area was the jail; its slate roof had not caught fire when burning objects, carried by the north wind, landed on it. So, slate roofs became a requirement. Now they were taking their toll of lives.

After the storm, newspapers would comment that during the period from five o'clock until the time the storm abated many Galvestonians were literally caught in a trap. People in houses along the beach had stayed too long.

In 1892, when this picture was taken, Galveston had more than 23,000 residents and was the largest city in Texas.

A 19th-century parade on 20th Street. The old City Hall can be seen at the north end of the street.

The Tremont, considered by many to be the finest hotel south of Saint Louis, was the favored stopping place of such important visitors as Ulysses Grant and Phil Sheridan.

Rising water covered the plush lobby of the Tremont during the height of the storm.

Courtesy of Mrs. Frank Walker

Alexander Coddou, employed at the telephone exchange, is seen crossing the sandy street in front of his home with his three young children. Coddou's house, like most others in Galveston, was raised above the ground to avoid flooding of the first floor during the seasonal "overflows." During the storm the house was demolished; Coddou and his three children were lost.

Rosenberg Library, Galveston

A popular pastime in Galveston in 1900 was the oyster roast. These derby-hatted, mustachioed citizens are stretching after the open-air feast.

For a nickel fare, a passenger on the Bath Avenue and Beach Line could enjoy a trolley ride over the surf.

"The longest wagon bridge in the United States" accommodated two-way traffic—until it was wrecked in the fateful September storm.

While these young men were gaily splashing in the surf on Sunday, September 2, the hurricane was already gaining strength some 200 miles south of Haiti.

Courtesy of Mrs. Frank Walker

Friday noon, September 7, 1900: Before entering a Galveston Beach restaurant Mr. and Mrs. Frank Walker snapped this picture of their horse. They didn't enjoy their steaks—angry waves and a skittish Bessie caused them to hurry through the meal and head for home.

U.S. Army Corps of Engineers, Galveston District

Moored on the east side of Galveston Island was the *General C. B. Comstock*. This dredge, then the largest vessel of its type in the world, was blown away from her berth, up the bay to Pelican Spit.

We Are Reaching Out

PACKARD'S LAUNDRY

MAILABLE EDITION.   TWELVE PAGES.

HOUSTON DAILY POST.

Bagging and Ties
G. C. Street & Co.,

XVITH YEAR—NO. 159.   HOUSTON, TEXAS, MONDAY, SEPTEMBER 10, 1900.   PRICE: 5 CENTS

THE FATE OF GALVESTON.

Mr. James G. Timmins Escaped from that City and Tells of the Hurricane's Effect.

ONE THOUSAND PERSONS DROWNED, KILLED OR MISSING, IT IS ESTIMATED.

Four Thousand Buildings Have Been Destroyed, Most of Them Residences; the Ritter Building Collapsed and Nine Prominent Men Were Killed—A Water Famine Now Threatens and Provisions Scarce.

GRAPHIC STORIES TOLD BY REFUGEES FROM GALVESTON.

On the Monday morning following the storm, Houston papers headlined "The Fate of Galveston" and carried first details of the disaster. Early estimates of property damage and loss of life were soon found to be too low.

Two views of Lucas Terrace at the turn of the century. Daisy Thorne Gilbert years ago wrote her own captions for these pictures; when her lettering faded, she wrote them in again.

At dawn on Sunday, when Zachary Scott viewed the destruction around St. Mary's Infirmary, he realized how fortunate he was to be alive.

Later Sunday morning, wearied Galveston citizens became stretcher-bearers as the ordeal of removing the dead began.

The corner of 14th and K after the storm. The house in the center, torn from its foundations, maintained this precarious balance after the waters receded.

wreckage of sailing vessels littered the shore, and the jumble of asts marked the havoc wrought by wind and sea.

Bodies were hauled away to barges on Monday for mass burial at sea. Many of them, improperly weighted, were washed ashore the next morning.

Shattered windows, fallen wires, and torn roofing still cluttered the downtown district a few days after the storm.

The skeletal tower and third floor of the City Hall drew a constant stream of onlookers before demolition work began.

The British steamship *Kendall Castle*, berthed on the north side of the city before the storm, was afterward stranded near Texas City in three feet of water.

NOTICE.

All Persons, Requiring Food will apply to the following Persons:

1st Ward, Mr Doyle, 10th, bet Market & P O
2nd Ward, Chas Wallis, 1426 P O St
3rd Ward, Jake Davis, 21st & Mechanic
4th Ward, Mr Torbert, Y M C A Building
5th Ward, Mart Royston, Y M C A Building
6th Ward, Mr Stenzel, 35th & H
7th Ward, Forster Rose, 34th & N½
8th Ward, Edmund Bourke & Sealy Hutchings, Garten Verein Bowling Alley, Ave N
9th Ward, C V Ousley, Tremont, bet N & N½
10th Ward, W F Coakley, 2018 O
11th Ward, John Goggan, St Mary's University
12th Ward, Dr West, 13th & P O

NOTE.—Water for stock can now be procured at Stand Pipe, 31st & H

THE COMMITTEE.

The shortage of edible food was a post-storm problem for Galvestonians. Although a committee was formed to distribute supplies, the looting of stores was hard to control.

To avoid another disaster, some Galveston citizens proposed raising the level of the city. A canal was dug, buildings were raised, sand was pumped in from the Gulf through pipes, and the first grade raising was finally completed in 1910.

Galvestonians also agreed to the construction of a sea wall and work was begun in 1902. The wall was completed in 1904 and proved its value during the 1915 hurricane.

Isaac Cline in later years. When he reached retirement age in 1931, New Orleans citizens successfully demanded that the Weather Bureau keep him on duty.

Courtesy of Mrs. Francis Cline Drake Thompson

Dr. Zachary Scott

Courtesy of Dr. Zachary Scott

Henry Ketchum, who moved away, later returned to Galveston with his family.

The Ketchum home after 1900, originally owned by Michel B. Menard, founder of Galveston.

Walter Bergstrom's home, built in 1886 at the cost of $664, survived the storm nobly: only two boards on the front porch had to be replaced.

A modern view of Galveston beach. Protected by the sea wall, it is a source of pride and enjoyment for Galveston.

The old Galveston City Hall in 1957. Minus tower and third floor, the remodeled building leaves no trace of the storm that nearly demolished the city on a weekend in September.

Some had not heeded warnings by the weathermen; others had not heard them. Now they were helpless. Most of them realized that their houses must soon be pounded to pieces, but they were afraid to leave.

At five-thirty Joseph Cline climbed the steps to his brother's front gallery. He motioned to several persons across the street to go into town. Then he went inside and discovered that his brother was already there. Also there was the contractor who had built the house; he and nearly fifty others had sought safety in the Cline residence.

Joseph Cline told his brother that the barometer reading was very low—somewhere below twenty-nine inches. When his brother advised him to take the horse and make his way to town, Joseph Cline refused to consider the offer.

About that time Henry Ketchum was nearing his home in a horse and buggy. He was returning from police headquarters, located at City Hall, where he had delivered a change of clothing to his father.

Chief Ketchum had telephoned his wife an hour or so earlier to ask for heavier clothes. She had assembled boots, a flannel shirt, and heavy trousers, and told Henry to take them to his father. He had left immediately in the buggy. The water in the street had not been very deep then, and he had encountered little difficulty in making the trip, although the rain had drenched him.

At police headquarters Henry Ketchum had given his father the clothing. Then, because there was so much excitement in the office, he had waited to see what was happening. When his father saw that Henry was still there, he ordered him home.

"Son," he said, "it's going to be pretty rough tonight."

Henry discovered that the trip home was much more difficult. He went out Broadway and turned left on 35th, a street that was covered with shell and graded higher than most other streets. Even on this comparatively high street the water was axle deep. Slate from the roof of Saint Patrick's Church, on 34th Street, blew all around him, but he was not hit. He reached his father's barn, took the harness off his horse, and put the animal in the corral. He never saw the horse after that.

Henry struggled half a block through chest-deep water to his house. As he neared it, he saw a floating doghouse lodged against a fence. On it was a Scottish terrier, chained to the doghouse. The dog barked to attract attention, but Ketchum was intent on saving himself. He has regretted ever since that he did not rescue the terrier.

When he was inside the house he called to his brother-in-law, Frank Eastman, to help him take up the carpet. It was tacked well, and difficult to remove; Kauffman, Meyers, and Company had laid it early that morning. While the two were working, water came onto the floor; it soaked the carpet. The two men admitted defeat.

"Oh, well," said Henry Ketchum, "let it go."

At this hour Fred Langben and his brother, at their desks at Jens Moller and Company, steamship agents, decided to head for home. They started off in their horse-drawn cart, going south on 23rd Street and turning left onto Sealy. At the intersection of Sealy and 22nd Street, wind blew the horse off its feet. The brothers got the animal up, but it would no longer pull the cart, so they had to lead the horse down Sealy.

On the north side of Sealy between 21st and 20th were the headquarters of the street railway company—general offices, car barns, and power plant. Over the power plant towered a brick smokestack. As the Langbens struggled down Sealy they saw, half a block ahead, the smokestack sway in the wind and fall.

Quickly they turned right on 21st. Fred Langben stepped off into a gutter and was up to his neck in water. After he had scrambled out, his brother shook his head and said, "Let's go back."

They turned west onto Broadway and north onto 23rd. On their way back to town the Langbens saw tin roofs rolling up and telephone poles falling. When they reached the downtown area once more, they put the horse in a livery stable and headed for the Tremont Hotel, talking vaguely of supper. A cornice blew off the hotel, and they decided they were not very hungry after all.

The Telephone Building, one block east of the Tremont, seemed the safest refuge. But the Langbens found one entrance locked, so they went around to the side. Fred's brother was a short distance ahead; when he turned the corner, wind blew him off his feet into the water. Fred had to help him up.

A man in the U. S. Corps of Engineers office, in the building, saw the two from a window. Fred Langben motioned to him to let them in. When he finally opened the door, they hurried inside.

Walter Grover, making his way back home in the storm, just missed seeing the Langbens leading their horse. Walking up 23rd, he too turned east on Sealy. Grover kept close to the houses on the north side of the street; the wind was still from the north-northeast.

"When I reached the carriage gates of the John Sealy residence, I paused for a few minutes to get my breath," Grover said later. "Clinging to the iron gates to hold myself against the wind and water, I saw the tin roof of the First Baptist Church a block away blow off and land across the street."

He crossed to the south side of the street to get farther away from the weakened building. When he was across 22nd he went back to the north side; the big synagogue of the Congregation B'nai Israel, on the northeast corner of 22nd and Sealy, was good protection.

After crossing 21st and going about half a block he saw a man, hanging to a yard fence, motioning him to the south side of the street. Grover went across.

When he reached the man, he found it was a friend, J. U. Rogers. Rogers told him the smokestack—the one that had collapsed while the Langbens watched—had fallen on the power house, killing several persons in that building. Rogers was afraid the power-house wall would collapse any time; Grover would have been walking under it. Even as Rogers was talking, the wall fell.

Grover finally reached home some time before six o'clock. He completed the trip by pulling himself along on fences and by swimming. He found his father, mother, and sister frantic; they had been certain he was dead. He also found that the chimney had fallen; locked doors were being blown open by the wind; water was pouring into the house. But Walter Grover did not leave home again during the storm.

After the Moores left their home it stood for a while; then it fell over against George Hoyle's house next door. This served to brace Hoyle's house against the wind and tide during the worst part of the storm and probably was the reason the Hoyle residence stood. (Until new siding was put on the house recently, the mark made by the

Moores' residence rubbing against it that Saturday afternoon was still visible.)

Many other houses near the Gulf were being pounded to bits by the storm and the debris. And the level of the water crept upward.

Five days later a Galveston *News* reporter was to interview an unidentified girl who told about her experience at this hour.

"Mamma and my eight little brothers and sisters were upstairs," said the youngster. "My papa is dead. I went down to see what the water was doing in the store—you see, we live upstairs, over the store. When I went down my brother was with me, and the water was halfway up the counter. But that didn't scare us. We had seen high water and heard high wind before.

"Well, we went back, but in a few minutes we were down again. The counter was floating. Brother said not to tell Mamma, but I did. Then I saw a house tumble down and we heard people crying. We got scared then and Mamma and I prayed. We prayed that one of us would not be drowned if the little children weren't drowned, because one of us would have to be their mamma."

On the west side, the house Pat Joyce and Lucian Minor were in was swept off its foundation and demolished.

"People all around me were making the air hideous with their cries," Joyce said later. Holding on to his niece, he saw Minor on some wreckage a few feet away. He heard Minor call to an aged colored man struggling in the water.

"Uncle, come over where I am," said Minor, who reached out to help the man.

Then Joyce's niece was swept from him. When Joyce looked up, Minor and the old man had disappeared.

"I was carried on and on with the tide," said Joyce. It carried him all the way to the mainland.

Zachary Scott had returned to Saint Mary's Infirmary after his unsuccessful attempt to get a train out of Galveston.

Between three and four o'clock streams of terrified people—those who could make it—had crowded into the hospital. Water was knee deep in the vicinity. By five-thirty it was five feet deep, and several persons lost their lives as they tried to reach the infirmary.

At about that time the force of the wind shattered the windows of the county building, a quarter of a block away. With their haven exposed to the storm, it was urgent that the patients be moved.

Scott rose to the challenge at once. For what seemed hours he carried patient after patient from the county building to the infirmary. With each trip the water rose perceptibly. By the time he finished the job, water was up to his shoulders.

Newspaper accounts later credited him with saving the lives of 200 patients. This is still a source of embarrassment to Scott, a retired doctor now living in Austin.

"There weren't two hundred patients in there," he says. "Besides, about fifty were ambulatory patients, and they walked over . . . I didn't carry them. I didn't do it all myself either; I couldn't have. Other men in the hospital helped me."

In mid-afternoon Sarah Littlejohn had seen an old man, who lived down the island, going home in a wagon. About

5:30 P.M. the Littlejohn family went into the living room, where Sarah's mother opened a blind.

"There we saw that same old man standing up to his waist in water," Sarah wrote later. "He was an old German, and we could not understand him very well. Mamma told him to come inside out of all that rain. It seemed to me that he could not understand us, for it took mamma a very long time to make him come inside.

"Papa at last found out that he was the father of one of his school boys. It surely did sound funny to hear him talk. He said he did not mind the water, but it was the wind he did not like. He was an old fisherman."

While Sarah Littlejohn was curiously eying the old German, someone in the crowd at the Tremont Hotel noted that water was knee deep in the lobby. The wind, as a former mayor of Galveston described it, was shaking the building "as a terrier would shake a rat."

At six o'clock Kate Hermann's grandmother, in a house seven blocks from the beach, was asking in German: "How are things outside?"

Eighteen persons, all women, were now gathered in the house, which belonged to Kate Hermann's aunt, Louisa Ahl.

"Grandma, I can't look," answered Miss Hermann in her limited, recently learned German. "I'm afraid to open the door." Only a month before, Miss Hermann had moved to Galveston from New Orleans to care for her eighty-year-old grandmother, who had been in the United States eight years and could not speak English.

Mrs. Ahl—a midwife who helped bring into the world 11,000 babies before she died—had returned from delivering a baby earlier in the afternoon; Miss Hermann had seen her coming down the street in the surrey when it was a block away. The horse, Fannie, was holding its head high, for the water then was already several feet deep. Miss Hermann had run out to help her aunt put the surrey in the carriage house and to unhitch the horse.

Shortly after, Kate had seen the poor animal struggling in fear. The water had risen, and Fannie obviously wanted to get in harness and leave. The horse's efforts so distressed Miss Hermann that she wanted to go out and open the surrey-house door. But her aunt would not hear of it.

"The water is getting too deep, and the waves are too high," said Louisa Ahl.

Now the eighteen women silently huddled together in Mrs. Ahl's house. No one dared even to open the door for a look outside.

They were afraid to go near the windows, which might at any moment shatter.

7 SATURDAY, 6:00–8:00 P.M.

A Warning of Death
and Destruction

AT SIX O'CLOCK, from Saint Mary's Cathedral, the Angelus rang out. To Father James M. Kirwin, rector, it sounded "not like a salutation of praise but a warning of death and destruction."

Suddenly the cathedral towers swayed violently. The two-ton bell that had just tolled the Angelus was torn from its iron bands and clasps and came crashing to the floor.

The Right Reverend Nicholas Gallagher, bishop of the diocese of Galveston, turned to Father Kirwin. Gesturing toward the several clergymen waiting in the room, he said quietly, "Prepare these priests for death."

Nearer the Gulf, the east and west portions of the city were being swept almost clean of residential and business structures.

Most survivors say that by the time it reached its peak, they had no hope of living through the storm. They watched as large brick buildings were flattened; as victims were cut, bruised, and killed by debris. Worst of all, they heard their own buildings creak and groan. Most had resigned themselves to dying, and hoped it would happen quickly.

A group of fifty hovered in a second-floor bedroom of a house near the beach. Other houses nearby had been demolished. Darkness was falling, intensifying the gloom which had blanketed the city since mid-afternoon.

Most waited in silence, but above the ceaseless wail of the storm several persons heard a small girl's voice pipe out:

"Mamma, how can I drown?"

Many survivors say they had planned to open their mouths and fill their lungs with water when death seemed imminent. But when that moment approached, the instinct of self-preservation often prevailed over the desire for a quick death. For some this served only to prolong the agony. Others miraculously saved themselves.

On the mainland, the boxcar in which C. A. Paschetag and sixteen others were cramped unexpectedly tipped over a few inches. Then it fell back on the track. Minutes later it did overturn but did not blow off the four-foot embankment on which it lay. Although the doors were shut, water seeped into the car.

"Where's this water coming from?" someone asked.

"It's rain water," answered another.

Paschetag tasted it, found that it was salty, and told the group that it was from the Gulf. Several men then cut a hole in the boxcar and saw that the water was indeed from the Gulf; the sea had reached the tops of the rails.

At this time, shortly after 6:00 P.M., while the wind was shifting toward the east, the tide was rising two and a half feet an hour in Galveston.

Perched atop the spire of Saint Patrick's Church, a Celtic cross that had withstood the fury of the storm all day now crashed to the earth. (This spire had been the tallest structure in the city, pointing some 200 feet into the sky.) So great was the noise of the wind that even people nearby did not hear it fall.

At this time Isaac Cline stood at his partly opened front door watching the water rise; it was already eight inches deep on the first floor. A sudden rise of four feet brought it above Cline's waist before he could move. The Gulf, now ten feet above the ground outside his home, brought the tide there to the record level of 15.2 feet.

This four-foot rise was a storm wave. Pushed ashore from the turbulent Gulf in advance of the storm's vortex, it swept over the southern section of the city, destroying houses in its path.

Florence Klaes, who was with her brother and the Allen family in the Letts' residence, believes that she saw this wave. She was looking out a door, opened to ease the pressure, and saw a gigantic swell carrying a horse on its crest. The animal was "rolling over and over," as a barrel would. The wave shook Letts' house violently when it struck, but the house did not fall.

S. O. Young, watching the storm from his second floor, also saw the wave.

"I went to a west window to watch the fence I had been using as a marker on the tide," he recalled later. "While I was looking I saw the tide suddenly rise fully four feet at one bound." Within minutes Young saw several houses on the south side of the street collapse.

Dr. John Mayfield, at the quarantine station, probably felt the effects of this wave. He was standing in the telephone room, at the front of the building, when a giant

swell pushed up the flooring. He dropped through between the joists, but his sons caught him. After that the
three went up to the attic and huddled together, holding
life preservers.

Eight and one-half miles down the island, Henry R.
Decie also was aware of the storm wave. He had taken his
wife and children to the home of a neighbor; they were
there when a sudden rise carried the house off its blocks.

"My wife and I were sitting on the foot of one of the
beds at that time," Decie said. "We felt the house quiver,
and my wife threw her arms around my neck and kissed
me. She said, 'Good-by. We are gone.'"

The house then broke up, and the Decies struggled to
escape.

"My baby boy was dead in my arms, killed by a falling
timber. Another wave came and swept the overhanging
house off my head. I looked around and discovered that
my wife was gone and the rest of the house was disin-
tegrating."

Decie grabbed a piece of wood and was swept across
the bay to the mainland. His family was drowned.

Clarence Howth observed the same storm wave from
his house near the beach.

Earlier in the day Howth had seen his tall chicken coop
in the back yard roll over; all the chickens were drowned.
An eight-foot fence around his garden was submerged in
water. As the wind blew the slate off his roof, new leaks
developed; he counted them as they appeared. The potted
ferns in the hallway caught the drops and began to look
as if they had been through a shower.

Incredulous at what he saw, Howth yet found himself
wondering what his wife would say when she saw her

lace curtains, her lace table coverings, and her soft feather pillows—all soaked. Mrs. Howth, in an upstairs bedroom with the newborn baby, was unaware of the severity of the storm.

Shortly before 6:00 P.M. Howth thought he saw the waters recede slightly. But immediately the sea began to rise again as the wind shifted. Shutters were torn off the house; windows were smashed. Neighboring houses collapsed quickly, so that by six o'clock it seemed every house to the east and west of his had been swept away. One of the nearest remaining houses was the Cline residence, but Howth could not see it; the evening was much too dark.

Mrs. Howth's father, Dr. John B. Sawyer, was upstairs looking after her now. Also in the house were her brother Ossapha, a nurse, and a maid. Howth called them to help move his wife from the east upstairs bedroom to a room on the west.

The five gently picked up the mattress on which Mrs. Howth and the baby lay, and moved them to a room on the leeward side.

"We thought nothing could save us," Howth said later. "For half an hour, it seemed, I paced the room, walking from the windows to the mattress where my wife lay, and back to the windows."

Leaks became streams, drenching everything. Then the four-foot storm wave helped cave in one side of the house. The family hurriedly carried Mrs. Howth and the baby up the steep stairs to the attic. The bedding was already soaked with salt water, and the roof was leaking "torrents."

When they reached the attic, the wind abated perceptibly. It was "a lull before the final onslaught," Howth thought.

Ossapha Sawyer knelt beside his sister and prayed that

God would save her. Dr. Sawyer, an old Confederate army surgeon from Tennessee, stood holding a cot upright against the attic window, trying to keep out the salty spray from waves that were actually breaking against the house at that height.

Howth also knelt beside his wife.

"I felt in three minutes we would all be dead," he recalled later.

Mrs. Howth called to her father. "Papa, are we going to die?"

"No, daughter," he answered. "It's almost over now."

Then Howth spoke to his wife. "Good-by, darling. We will meet in heaven."

"I'm not afraid to die."

Howth remembered later that the wind then shifted again.

"Stay with the house as long as there's a piece of it!" old Dr. Sawyer shouted. "If she stands this five minutes it will all be over."

Those were his last words; the rest of the house fell.

"The crash threw me away from my wife, and I sank underneath the water," Howth said. "I thought I, too, would die. I opened my mouth and sucked in water so it would be over quickly, but instinct replaced the urge to die. I struggled to the surface."

Howth was carried southwestward down the beach. He lodged against what he thought was a house, but closer observation showed that it was only one room of a wrecked building. This debris afforded some protection from the wind and rain, and he stayed there a while. Forced off by the current, he then grabbed a window frame and floated on it. Where, he did not know, but he thought he was later carried out into the Gulf and back.

At Morgan's Point, Mrs. Curtin and her children had moved into the nearby residence of W. H. Coyle. Randle Pittman, their servant, stayed in the Curtin house to look after things. As the storm grew worse Mrs. Curtin wished that Pittman had not been left behind, but there was no way of calling him now. Then she saw him making his way through the wind and water to reach them.

Mrs. Curtin says she will never forget how rough the sea became. "The waves looked like the sides of huge elephants. Every wave that came in raised the house up, and each time we thought, 'This is the last one now.'" But the house was well anchored and it did not collapse.

At Port Bolivar, lighthousekeeper Claiborne believed that the only safe place now was in the lighthouse itself. With some of the men, he stretched ropes between the house and the light tower, a distance of fifty feet. They struggled against the wind, which now was strong enough to sweep a man off his feet. Slowly each person in the Claiborne residence made his way to the lighthouse and went on up the winding iron stairway until the last one was inside.

In Unger's grocery, some of the men braced the walls with beams they had found floating outside, and they nailed shut the doors and windows. Others chopped holes in the floor so that the water coming through would help hold the store on its foundation. Others in the room prayed. Ephraim Moore, who was helping to brace the walls, swore and said, "It's too late to pray now. Get to work."

The water rose to such depth on the first floor that everyone except Mrs. Moore went upstairs. She stayed below, fearing that the second floor would be blown away. She tried to avoid the rising water by standing on top of a barrel containing sugar. But the water dissolved the sugar, and Mrs. Moore, a stout woman, suddenly found herself standing inside the barrel when the top caved in. Her husband pulled the barrel off over her head, and she decided to go upstairs too.

There, Jim Moore sat with his father next to a window. "If the house goes, I'll throw you out," his father told him. Jim Moore does not remember being especially worried by the prospect. "If we have to go that way," he reasoned then, "we'll have to go."

Y.M.C.A. secretary Palmer had taken Isaac Cline's advice. He stayed in his home. Some of the people who had come there for shelter helped him to carry the first-floor furniture and carpets upstairs. At seven o'clock the front door was blown in, and water—two feet deep—splashed over the first floor. Rain and spray splattered the parlor, but the crowd, now upstairs, remained comparatively dry.

Palmer prayed, and his son Lee prayed too. Palmer later remembered the boy's words:

"Dear Jesus, make the waters recede, and give us a pleasant day tomorrow to play, and save my little dog Youno."

The situation was now desperate. High winds broke the windows. Plaster fell in great chunks from the ceiling. Rain poured in through the now-shattered roof. One of the men thought that he would be safer in the bathroom, and immediately twelve of the group followed him into that space.

"I took Lee in my arms, and with Mrs. Palmer's arm around my neck I braced my back against the door, to keep it from blowing in," Palmer recalled.

As soon as the front part of the house was carried away,

the rest of it began to settle slowly. Soon Palmer felt water inching up his legs. One of the neighbors, realizing that what was left of the house was about to collapse, opened the bathroom window and called to the others to jump out after him. Ten leaped, most of them to their deaths. The Palmers were left, trying to keep their balance in the rising water.

"I grabbed the shower pipe with my left hand, still holding Lee with my right arm. Mrs. Palmer grabbed the pipe with her right hand. Lee, holding me around my neck, asked, Papa, are we safe? I felt the water rise around my body to my neck and almost to my mouth.

"Just then the whole north end of the house fell in; the roof settled on us, and we went down into the water together.

"I thought, it takes so long to die. I was possibly unconscious for a time. Then I had another thought: I wonder what heaven will be like?"

Palmer lost his wife and son. He was caught by the current and thrown onto some drift. For three hours after that he lay on top of a floating shed, cast about at the mercy of the storm.

"As I drifted," he said later, "these words came to me: 'When thou passeth through the waters I will be with thee.'"

At seven o'clock First Mate Ledden of the *Comino*, which was tied up at a wharf, noted that the ship's barometer read 28.30 inches. He also wrote in the log:

"Wind blowing terrific, and steamer bombarded with large pieces of timber, shells, and all manner of flying debris from the surrounding buildings."

The bombardment made a floating wreck of the *Comino*.

While the crew huddled below deck hoping they would live to see England again, a board four feet long and six inches wide was blown through one of the inch-thick iron plates.

Every ship in port was battling for survival. The *Taunton,* which had got up steam early in the day, met with a force generated by nature that was too much for mere engines. While the *Comino,* on the wharf front, was being battered by flying debris, the *Taunton's* anchors lost their grip on the bottom of Bolivar Roads, and the ship was set adrift. Its progress was slowed for a few minutes by the anchors as they caught here and there on the bottom. But this soon caused the anchor chains to snap, and the ship and her crew were at the mercy of the hurricane.

Captain Page of the *Taunton* later told quarantine officer Mayfield that when the vessel was being driven before the wind he was certain the ship would smash the quarantine station to bits. Just before she reached Mayfield's station, however, the wind changed direction enough so that the *Taunton* cleared it.

She was tossed about near the jetty for some time. Then she was sent by an east-southeast wind at tremendous speed over the rock jetty, across Pelican Island, up the bay into shallow water. When the storm was through with Captain Page's ship, she lay aground at Cedar Point, about thirty miles from where she had been anchored.

It mattered little whether ships were at anchor or alongside a wharf. In the first case anchor chains were snapped. In the second case mooring lines were parted. But the result was nearly always the same. The *Hilarious* went aground near Bolivar Roads. The *Comstock* had already been blown away from her berth at the coal wharf to Pelican Spit.

Captain Storm had fought all Saturday to keep the *Roma* at Pier 15. Both anchors and every line she had, rope and steel, were out. But the stern mooring post gave way, and the wind forced the ship's stern into the stream. At 7:15 P.M. the *Roma* broke the last of her bonds when the anchors parted from the chains. The ship was carried up the channel broadside to the current.

Captain Storm had no clear recollection of what happened after that. He did remember shouting to his crew that it was useless to try to fetch her up, but it is doubtful that any of his men heard him over the roar of the wind. The ship careened into the *Kendal Castle*, then went broadside through the three railroad bridges linking the island with the mainland. She finally came to a halt between the last railroad bridge and the wagon bridge.

When the *Roma* crashed into the *Kendal Castle* she loosened its mooring lines. Later the small Norwegian *Guyller* also piled into the *Kendal Castle*, whereupon she too went adrift. Driven by the hurricane, the ship was sent across Pelican Island and into shallow water near Texas City. The *Guyller*, meanwhile, was stranded midway between Pelican Island and Virginia Point.

The *Alamo* and *Red Cross* had broken loose about six o'clock. Both were flung across the channel, where they collided on the opposite side. By seven-fifteen they were aground near each other on the edge of Pelican Island. The *Benedict* was also aground across the channel, opposite Pier 18.

The *Comino* and *Norna* were fortunate. They stayed at their berths, but both were extensively damaged.

On the island even the sturdiest buildings were falling now.

In Saint Mary's Orphanage, everyone—including Sister Elizabeth and the workman who had been sent for her—had moved to the second floor. They had remained in the chapel, on the first floor of the girls' wing, until the rising water forced them upstairs. From their second-floor vantage point they watched, with horror, as the boys' wing collapsed.

Mother Superior Camillus sent one of the workmen to a storeroom for some clothesline, which she and the nuns cut into short pieces. Then they tied the orphans together and fastened them to their cinctures. They were as well prepared for the inevitable as they thought they could be.

Some time between seven and eight o'clock, while the hurricane was tossing the ships about like toys, the roof fell in on the orphanage group. Albert Campbell, thirteen, and Francis Bolenick, fourteen, evidently thrown through a window, clung to a piece of drift. Will Murney, thirteen, struggled out of the wreckage alone. They were probably the only survivors of Saint Mary's Orphanage, although there was talk later that another child had been saved.

Murney was swept along by the current for a few minutes; then he grabbed the top of a tree. Campbell and Bolenick were already clinging to it. The tree was caught in the masts of a wrecked schooner, the *John S. Ames.*

The three clung to the tree the rest of the night. Once Campbell cried that he was drowning, and Murney tied him to the tree with a piece of rope he had found in the wreckage. Later the tree broke loose from the masts of the schooner and carried the boys ashore.

At about the same time Mrs. Carrie M. Hughes, her young daughter Mattie, Mrs. Eliza Williams, and her daughter Hattie were already floating in the Gulf—on, of all things, part of a ceiling.

"The wall of broken houses and debris struck our house and crushed the lower part," Mrs. Hughes recalled. "As the house settled I felt the ceiling touching the back of my head, and the water was just under my chin." Mattie's arms were around her mother's neck.

Then the roof blew over their heads, and they grabbed the wreckage that carried them out into the Gulf.

"It was the most intense cold I ever felt," Mrs. Hughes said. "We thought we would freeze. We lay there as close to each other as we could get, to keep warm. Our thirst was terrible, but when we opened our mouths to let the rain moisten our tongues it was as briny as the Gulf. The rain stung as if it were hail; some say it was hail, but the terrible wind prevented us from telling whether it was or not."

On one occasion Hattie Williams raised up to get a firmer grip on the wreckage, and the wind stripped off her clothes.

Although the Hughes residence had fallen, the home of H. B. Cullum, on the west side near Fort Crockett, was still standing. A few soldiers from the fort, some with their wives, had come to the house earlier in the day. Shortly after seven-fifteen everybody collected in the library, and several soldiers were bracing themselves against the folding doors to hold them in place against the wind. They had heard the roof blow off half an hour earlier, and now they were alarmed to hear a mass of debris—which proved to be large beams from Fort Crockett—strike the house. The house was knocked off the seven-foot-high brick piers that supported it. The library was crushed in by the fall, and part of its floor was covered by several feet of water.

"We were trapped in a space about two feet between the ceiling and the floor," Cullum said. "I found myself pinned under one of the folding doors. I was helped out by a sergeant named Snyder, who pulled me into the dining room. It hadn't settled so much."

Cullum then helped his wife into the dining room; and twenty-one others in the group managed to crawl in. One of the soldiers who had been standing beside Cullum was killed.

Someone in the group saw a broken window. With the idea of getting as far away as possible from the water, each person went out the window and up the side of the tilted house into a second-floor room. The roof was gone, and a bedroom wall had fallen; it was leaning against a writing desk. The wall was as high above the water as they could get, and most of them climbed onto it. There they stayed, said Cullum, "holding on with both hands, expecting every moment to be thrown into the water as the house kept going to pieces. The raindrops were like shot striking us."

Ordinarily, the day force of patrolmen came off duty at seven. Usually they reported in at the station, but it was an impossibility that night.

Water, five feet deep, raced down the two narrow streets that ran along the sides of the city hall; it swept planks, sheds, telephone poles—everything—before it. Inside the building were 400 refugees, many of them terrified, and four policemen—Chief Ketchum, Rowan, Byrd, and Johnson. Ketchum was having great difficulty in maintaining order.

At this hour a thirty-foot sailboat carrying E. F. Gerloff and nineteen others capsized. When Gerloff's family and several neighbors had realized that his house was about to fall, they had taken to the boat as a last resort. After

the boat overturned, Gerloff never again saw his wife and
their two children, his mother, two brothers, and two sis-
ters-in-law. He was trapped in the cabin, with just enough
air space between the water and the cabin deck above him
to breathe. He was to stay there twenty-four hours.

At this hour, too, water was nearly ten feet deep around
the house to which Florence and Ralph Klaes and the
Allens had fled; forty-eight persons were gathered there.
The house had been intended for use as a store. Among
its fixtures were a high counter and shelves around the
walls. Upstairs was an attic.

Ralph Klaes kept out of the water, which was several
feet deep on the first floor, by hanging on to a shelf in the
north corner of the room. His sister was standing on the
counter. With them were Mr. and Mrs. Allen and Claude,
and Mr. and Mrs. Louis Moore and their four girls—
Cecilia, Loraine, Vera, and Mildred. (The youngest was
a baby just beginning to stand.) The Moores had started
to town, but they could not get there. Now they were
sitting on a shelf, near Ralph Klaes, with their children.

Above, on top of the ceiling joists, were others, among
them Bill Letts and his family.

The roof had blown off, and the water was still rising.
Letts poked a sheet down for Ralph Klaes. He grabbed it
and pulled himself up into what was left of the attic. He
was there when the house, already weakened by the storm
wave that Florence Klaes had seen earlier, broke up.

The ceiling split, and Ralph was separated from the
others. He was carried westward across the street, where
the part of the ceiling to which he clung was lodged
against the south side of a house. The part to which Letts
and his relatives clung went to the north side of the same
house; they were all drowned. Unable to swim a stroke,

Klaes hung on to the ceiling until it went to pieces and he went under the water. He scrambled up, "like a cat," and grabbed other debris. Two more times he went under until, vomiting salt water, he grabbed a long plank.

Klaes wrapped his arms and legs around the plank. This one, he resolved, was not going to get away from him. The plank was propelled westward—almost due west, he remembers clearly—by the racing water. Sometimes it rolled over and over, but he hung on. Each time he came up gasping for breath; then he vomited the water.

Klaes was carried a mile and a quarter west to a grove of salt cedar trees. They ranged from twelve to fourteen feet tall, but the tops were just poking out of the water. When Ralph hit the limbs he grabbed one and clamped his legs around the submerged part, clutching the top with his hands. The plank on which he had been riding was swept on westward.

Florence Klaes, thrown off the counter into the water when the house fell, saw Allen, with young Claude hanging around his shoulders, swept through the double front door. They were "spun around like a top." She also saw the Louis Moores, a child under each arm, go under. Then Florence Klaes went under water herself.

She felt a hand grab her ankle and hold her beneath the surface.

"I was breathing in water. Everything was turning black when I kicked loose from that hand and came up."

Rising to the surface, she hit a window or a glass door and cut herself; the scars are still on her hand. She climbed on floating debris and sat up; a few yards away she saw three persons crouched on a piece of wreckage "that must have been the side of a house." Then she was hit on the forehead by a piece of wood and was knocked unconscious. When she recovered she sat up again and was knocked flat by something that hit the back of her head. Regaining consciousness the second time, she felt a tree limb brush against her. Florence Klaes grabbed it and hung on. After a few minutes she could see a boy clinging to another limb about twenty feet away.

George Trebosius, the Galveston *News* mailing-room employee, and his family were in their third house of the afternoon.

They had left their own home when water was waist deep around it, and had gone to a neighbor's two-story house. Then, when that one seemed about to fall, they moved to a rambling one-story house built over three lots. Now this one, too, appeared to be on the verge of collapsing. Trebosius, in a panic to escape, broke a window with his fist. Going out, he stepped on some of the jagged glass.

He clung to branches of a tree just outside the house. With him was his wife, who held a six-year-old girl, sister of a friend. A large swell engulfed them all and leveled the house. When Trebosius was able to look again he saw that his wife and the girl were gone. (Later he learned that he had also lost his brother, two sisters, a brother-in-law, and four nieces and nephews.)

Meanwhile the storm was demolishing the rooming house where Mary Lothringer, her mother, and several others were gathered in the dining room. When the undermined foundation crumbled, the house settled into the water. Two large safes—cupboards for dishes—toppled over, one on top of the other. People scrambled upon them, and still they were in water nearly neck deep.

A man in the crowd noticed something against a window. Making his way through the water for a close look, he found it was a cistern that had floated off its foundation. The top was too high to reach, but a two-by-four had been driven straight through the cistern, and one end of the board was within reach. He grabbed it, pulled himself up, and saw that the cistern was empty. He twisted a tablecloth into a makeshift rope and tied it to the two-by-four. The others struggled up the rope and then plopped into the cistern. Nails on the inside ripped their clothing as they fell to the bottom. Nine persons, including the Lothringers—and a woman with a nine-month-old baby—were to spend the entire night there.

A few minutes after 7:15 P.M. John Blagden, alone in the Weather Bureau office, noted that the barometer had dropped to a new low of 28.48 inches. It was then lower than any previous official barometer reading made by the U. S. Weather Bureau.

The wind was now coming from the east. Minutes later Blagden saw that the barometer had begun to rise. The center of the hurricane, he knew, was passing Galveston—several miles to the southwest.

At 7:30 P.M. water was fifteen feet deep around Isaac Cline's residence. The crowd there was jammed into a room on the windward side; the Cline brothers had reasoned that they would be on the top wall of the building as it fell, if it were blown over. Joseph Cline warned the group that the house would collapse at any moment. They were horrified to see, from their second-floor refuge, wreckage smashing against nearby houses.

The Cline house, however, still stood after those on every side of it had been demolished. But debris had already ripped off the two-story porches at the front and rear and finally a great mass of wreckage was hurled against the house.

"We probably would have weathered the storm," Isaac Cline said years after it was all over, "but a trestle was torn from its moorings and the storm swells drove this wreckage against the house."

Rails held the trestle together, so that it was a 200-foot-long instrument of destruction. The rails protruded fifty feet from each end. As the trestle moved, it had gathered wreckage, which was piled high on it, and it had upset one raft carrying twenty-five persons. Then the trestle hit the side of Cline's house.

Joseph Cline had taken a position near a window. With him were Isaac Cline's two eldest daughters, Allie May and Rosemary. Isaac Cline was with his wife and youngest daughter, Esther Ballew, near the center of the room.

Joseph Cline remembered the moment clearly.

"Strangely enough, I didn't feel unduly excited. In fact, I was almost calm. I kept thinking of an uncle aboard a sinking ship who saved himself by getting on a plank when the vessel went under. He drifted five miles to shore."

The crowd, however, became panicky. Joseph Cline remembered that most of them began to sing. Some, hysterical, were crying and moaning; others knelt in prayer. Then the terrified people felt the house shudder and move off its foundation. It was actually afloat. Looking like a listing ship, it began to roll over in the water. Joseph Cline grabbed the hands of his two nieces and, back-first, he lunged toward the window. He smashed through the glass and the storm shutters, and the momentum carried all three through the opening. The house rolled on over, "rocked a bit, and rose on the surface of the flood." The two youngsters and Joseph Cline were alone on the top side.

A block away from the Clines, S. O. Young had seated himself in a chair and made himself as comfortable as possible. He was at least alone, with no responsibilities. "But I was a complacent fool not to be afraid," he admitted after the storm.

About seven-thirty, just before the Cline residence fell, Young had heard a thumping against the east side of his house. It seemed to be coming from the vicinity of his bedroom downstairs. He found a candle and lighted it. Then he started for the first floor to investigate the dreadful noise. When he reached the stairs, he saw by the dim light of his candle that the Gulf was nearly to the top step.

Young put down the candle and felt his way to the front door that opened to his second-story gallery. Opening it, he was blown several feet back into the hall. Easing himself toward the door again, he grasped first the doorknob, then the side of the open door, then a blind on the outside. Clinging with both hands for support, he pulled himself out onto the gallery.

"It was impossible to face the wind, and the roar was awful," he said. "To the right and left as far as I could see only my house and that of my next-door neighbor, Mr. Youens, were left standing. We were practically out in the Gulf."

Minutes later he saw his neighbor's house begin to move. It turned partly around, and for a few seconds it hung there as if suspended. Then it rose out of the water, looking like "a huge steamboat," and was swept from Young's sight.

"I knew Mr. Youens had his family with him," Young said later. "Perhaps you can imagine my feeling."

By the time Youens' house had disappeared the water had reached the second story of Young's house; now it was pouring through the door where Young stood. The wind that lashed at him, he recalled, was like a Niagara Falls; it did not come in gusts.

One of the gallery posts blew away and struck Young, cutting his head, badly bruising his shoulder, and knocking him insensible for a few seconds. When he recovered he noticed that the constant jarring and shaking had loosened the door. He saw that he could tear it loose and use it for a raft when the house fell.

"The other posts and the gallery railing then blew away, and the wind flung the top of the gallery over the house. Then the gallery itself floated away, and I was left hanging against the front of the house with one foot inside the door.

"I was beginning to think my house would never go, when I felt it yielding. I took a firm hold on the door, placed both feet against the house, and exerted my full strength. I tore the door loose, and as the house went I kicked myself as far away from it as possible."

Young saw his house rise out of the water several feet, just as his neighbor's had done. Then it was "whisked away," and he was on his own in the storm.

"The surface of the water was almost flat. The wind beat it down so that there wasn't the slightest suspicion of a wave. The current impelled by the wind was terrific. Almost before I felt I had started I was over the Garten Verein, four blocks away."

For hours Young clung to the board, and he had no idea where the current carried him. He finally grounded at

34th and Avenue M½, fifteen blocks from where his house had stood. During that time he witnessed more destruction than he had ever seen before.

Debris crashing against buildings had caused much of the destruction. The first structures to be beaten down were those nearest the Gulf. Most of the buildings in that area were frame residences, far less substantial than those in the center of town.

The wreckage from the first street of demolished buildings then was thrown against the next. They, too, fell and added more wreckage for the storm to hurl at the next block of buildings. This was the pattern of the destruction of much of Galveston. But many houses between Avenues M and P withstood the pounding, and the Gulf's totally destructive advance toward the center of the city finally was halted.

Isaac Cline had seen his brother break through the window when the house rolled over slowly in the water. Then a dresser had skidded across the room and pinned him and his wife and youngest daughter against a mantel. They were carried under water and held there. Cline was certain that he would drown; his last thought was that at least he had done his duty to the end. He decided to take water into his lungs quickly.

Above the water, only a few feet from where Isaac Cline was trapped, Joseph Cline and his two nieces clung to the outside wall of the capsized house, which had not yet completely broken up. It was afloat, with the wall to which they clung out of the water.

Joseph and the girls saw that no one else who had been in the room with them only minutes before had succeeded in getting out; as far as he could tell, the only way of escape was through the window he had smashed.

Rain continued to pour down, drenching Cline and his two nieces, but the clouds had broken in spots. Occasionally the moon shone through.

Cline, remembering the adage that drowning persons will seize any object within reach, crawled over to the window he had broken and called into the darkness below, "Come here! Come here!" Then he lowered his legs through the smashed window and swung them back and forth in the water.

There was no sign from the darkness beneath him that anyone was still alive.

The wall on which the three crouched was pitching like a ship. One second it would rise several feet out of the water; the next moment it would drop to the surface. Slowly the house was breaking up.

The wreckage that had entangled Isaac Cline trapped his wife and carried her to the bottom. Cline himself had no idea how he got to the surface, but when he regained consciousness his head was above water and surging timbers were brushing about his chest. His six-year-old daughter, on a shattered piece of the roof, was trying to raise herself. A plank lying across her back held her down. Cline came to his senses in time to see a piece of wood being blown toward her; he raised his hand and deflected it. Then he groped in the debris-littered water for his wife, but he could not find her.

Isaac Cline crawled onto the piece of roof and took his daughter in his arms. Is this all that's left of us? he asked himself. For five minutes he was resigned to an affirmative answer. Then he made out the forms of three figures bent low on some pitching debris about 100 feet to windward.

"Who's there?" he shouted into the storm. At the same time the voice of one of his daughters called, "Who are you?"

The two groups were reunited about thirty minutes after the house fell.

People in the second-floor room of the Union Passenger Station heard buildings crashing to earth, and they glanced up anxiously at water seeping through their own weakened plaster. There were times, Jesse Toothaker remembers, when it seemed to him the wind would almost cease blowing; however, it always came back "with renewed fury."

But in a room in the Cotton Exchange Building, A. J. Beckway was fast asleep. Beckway, a clerk employed by S. O. Young, had spent all Saturday afternoon with another employee, A. S. Johnson, trying to save the windows in the building. He had secured windows and shutters as well as he could; then he had gone back to those the wind blew open and tried to fasten them again. The wind, however, had opened shutters faster than he could close them. It had, in fact, blown many of them out completely. Beckway and Johnson gave it up as an impossible job.

The two young men then had gone to the guest room in the northwest corner of the building and flopped on the bed, exhausted. Soon they were joined by two Cotton Exchange messenger boys looking for a place to wait out the storm.

"We may have chewed the fat for a while," Beckway recalls now, "but pretty soon we dropped off to sleep."

John Hopkins, superintendent of Galveston public schools, also went to bed early. Alone in his home, only a few blocks from the downtown section, he had chopped holes in his floor with an ax so the water would weight down the house. The exertion had made him thirsty, and he went into the kitchen for a drink of water.

Fumbling around in the darkness, he found a bottle of beer, but he could not locate an opener. He broke off the top of the bottle and drank the beer. Then he went upstairs and went to sleep almost immediately, little realizing the immensity of the storm outside.

Fifteen blocks from Hopkins' residence, the nurse at John Sealy Hospital was adding another hurried paragraph to her letter:

"Darkness is overwhelming us, to add to the horror. Dearest, I reach out my hand to you—my heart—my soul."

8 SATURDAY, 8:00 P.M.—DAWN
SUNDAY

Clear of Water

JESS AND BILL SIMPSON, who had anchored the schooner
Hard Times in Galveston Bay, discovered that the spot
where they were anchored, north of Pelican Island, was
not at all the safe place they had thought. It was, instead,
probably the worst place they could have selected. When
sea water covered Galveston it submerged Pelican Island
also.

By eight o'clock, with the wind coming from a more
southerly direction, the Simpsons had become fully aware
of an unforeseen danger of their location. Though their
schooner had not been struck by steamers blown adrift,
it was threatened by the wreckage that was now being
swept from Galveston across Pelican Island by the wind
and sea.

"A house roof came straight at us at one time during
the evening," Bill Simpson remembers. "Our boat went up
on one of the giant swells and came crashing down on top
of the roof. The boat wasn't damaged by this, but the roof
was smashed to pieces."

The Simpsons, by now certain that the *Hard Times*
would soon sink and that they would surely die, heard in
the darkness more wreckage slamming against the sides
of their boat.

118

"We could also hear people screaming and crying out for help," Bill recalls in a tone that reflects the terror he experienced that night. "It seems I can hear them yet."

The Simpsons could hardly see any of those persons who, in the blackness, were being swept past the pitching schooner to their fate; but the brothers tied a piece of lead to the end of a rope and hopefully cast it in the direction of the screams.

"During the whole night we reached only five boys, who were able to hang on to the line until we pulled them aboard," Bill says. "They ranged in ages from ten to fourteen. All of them were so exhausted and scared they didn't answer any of our questions, so we just wrapped them in blankets and put them in our bunks."

More than fifty persons inside Bolivar Lighthouse had been gradually moving up the stairs as the water rose. The doorway was about eight feet high, and occasional swells filled the entrance completely.

A man on a lower step kept shouting to those above him. "Move up a step, please," he implored. "You wouldn't want a man to drown before your eyes!"

Up another few feet moved the group, but the water followed them.

Another man, who had a small boy with him, had become frenzied. "If this storm gets any worse I'm going to cut my throat, then cut Walter's," he kept repeating.

The lighthousekeeper's wife finally laughed him into silence by asking others how the man would be in any condition to cut Walter's throat.

The mechanism that turned the lighthouse beam had ceased to operate, and Claiborne ascended the winding stairway to work it by hand.

"I don't know who'll see it, but I'll help you turn it," Mrs. Claiborne told her husband. As she climbed the stairs, the tower swayed.

The light at Fort Point, on the island across Bolivar Roads, was bright. Old Colonel Anderson had as usual gone up at the hour of sunset (that Saturday night it was at 6:33 P.M.) and put the brass kerosene lamp within the circular magnifying lens. He had drawn aside the linen curtains that hung around the glass enclosure during the day, and watched the light cast its strong beam across the stormy Gulf. Then he had gone below.

Now, about eight o'clock, spray was blowing over the top of the tower, and Anderson went up once more to be certain that his light was burning. He had just come through the small opening in the tower floor when the wind blew in one of the thick glass panes on the northeast side. A piece of glass struck Anderson in the face and left him stunned and bleeding. Then the light went out.

Even Anderson saw the hopelessness of trying to relight it. He went below.

Mrs. Anderson dressed her husband's wounds, and the two sat quietly in the parlor awaiting the end they were sure was to come. Even above the roar of the wind they could hear the metallic clanking of the rails that had been torn from the track on the jetty and were now scraping against the steel supports of their lighthouse.

Some time after 8:00 P.M. water reached its maximum depth over Galveston Island. It was 15.7 feet deep at Henry Schutte's grocery on the east side, 15.6 feet at Saint Mary's Infirmary a block away. Downtown the depth was 12.1 feet at the Y.M.C.A. building, and 10.5 feet at Union Passenger Station.

The home of Edward R. Girardeau, at 1613 Broadway, was situated virtually on top of the highest point in the city, and water was a foot deep on the elevated first floor. (Strangely enough, the level of the water was not uniform throughout the city—possibly because of the effect of the wind, possibly because wreckage in some areas acted as a dam and held the water at a higher level.)

Nobody ever knew exactly how deep the water was at Lucas Terrace. By eight o'clock the hinges of both doors had broken, and the men in the group had to hold them up against the sea. The men took turns resting: one at a time.

Most of the ceiling had been destroyed nearly two hours before. The Gulf swept into the tiny bedroom, breaking against the walls that remained and pouring over the tops of them. Those in the room gasped for breath after each inundation. They had difficulty staying on their feet. Daisy Thorne held a bag containing twenty five-dollar gold-pieces with which she and Dr. Gilbert had planned to buy furniture. As it became more and more difficult to stand up and hold on to her relatives, she tossed the bag away.

On Morgan's Point, far up the bay, Mrs. Curtin saw a light pass the window. Ruth Curtin saw it too.

"Somebody has come for us!" Mrs. Curtin exclaimed happily, but she soon realized it must have been a kerosene lamp in a floating house. The swells continued to slap against the Coyle house, where the Curtins had taken refuge, and the winds rocked it violently.

At this hour nearly 1000 terrified persons were gathered in the massive Ursuline Convent, ten blocks from the beach. A ten-foot wall around the convent had crumbled, and people, animals, and debris were being washed against the walls of the building. Many persons were taken into the convent, including four expectant mothers who gave birth to children that night while lying on cots in nuns' cells. The babies were baptized immediately; few persons expected them—or anyone else in the trembling building— to live through the night.

After the Clines had been reunited about eight o'clock they were forced to keep moving from one sinking piece of debris to another. Then the wreckage of a house bore down upon them. The Cline brothers reached for the top of it, and their weight was enough to pull it down far enough so that they and the children could scramble onto it.

For two hours the five huddled on the wreckage. They were probably taken out to sea; for a while they could see no houses, no lights, and no other persons. Then they were swept back upon the island.

"To avoid being killed by the flying timbers we placed the children in front of us, our backs to the wind, and held planks to our backs to distribute the blows the wind-driven debris was showering upon us," Isaac Cline recalled.

Occasionally one of the brothers would be knocked completely off the raft and would have to fight his way back through the water. Drifting back toward the city, they heard cries for help from the second floor of a two-story house in their path. Their makeshift raft rammed the house and collapsed it; Isaac was hit by falling lumber.

Joseph Cline turned his attention to his brother and was relieved to discover that he apparently was not badly hurt. Then he noticed a small girl struggling in the water, grabbed at her clothes, and pulled her out—thinking she was his youngest niece knocked off the wreckage. Several minutes passed before he realized that Isaac Cline's six-year-old daughter was still with him. The girl was a stranger.

By 8:15 P.M. Sarah Littlejohn and the others, except for the old German fisherman, were upstairs in the house. The old man would not go up; he sat downstairs in a rocking chair with his feet propped against the front door, water all around him. Suddenly the front door blew open and the wind tossed the old man across the hall.

Littlejohn went downstairs to help the man close the door, but it blew open again. Littlejohn began to look for some nails. Finding none on the lower floor, he went up to the second-floor bathroom and took apart some shelves. From these he salvaged a few.

The rest of the family moved into the bathroom.

"Mamma stood on the edge of the bathtub and looked out of the window," Sarah wrote later. "My brother, Harry, sat on a little box where papa brushes his shoes. Harry was leaning against the wall. My youngest sister, Liska, sat on a little chair with her head bent over on her pillow.

"At first my eldest sister, Fleda, and I sat up on the clothes basket, but after a while I got down and sat in the stationary wash stand. The ceilings were leaking badly and the water felt so cold. We all were wet because the water was dripping down on us."

When Littlejohn opened the bathroom door to return downstairs with his nails, a strong draft blew the window out.

"We did not know that it would go so quick, but when papa opened the door mamma said, 'There goes the window pane,' and it went as quick as lightning, almost. Mamma was standing right at it."

Littlejohn nailed the front door shut and then returned. Later Sarah thought she heard someone crying outside, not far away. Still later, when she was able to look outside, she saw the bodies of a man and a young girl in the yard.

Shortly after eight-thirty the wind, now blowing from the southeast with a force that must have exceeded 110 miles an hour, shattered the east windows on the top floor of the city hall, and the crowd below nearly stampeded. Collapse of the front part of the building closely followed. Police Chief Ketchum climbed upon his desk and stood there, waving a billy. By threatening to wade in on the crowd if order was not restored, he succeeded in quieting most of the people.

But then the walls of the third story fell and, with a frightening roar, the roof tumbled. The crowd went wild with hysteria. Ketchum remembered afterward that someone near him sang in a voice loud enough to be audible above the din: "Praise God, from whom all blessings flow . . ."

In the Cortes residence, where a birthday party had been planned for Saturday, son-in-law Michaelis stacked patent-medicine boxes against the doors.

Frank Walker, who had reached the house in the afternoon, was wearing some dry clothes that had belonged to the late Henry Cortes, Sr. Walker, a rather large man, had split the back of the trousers and laced them with cord to make them fit.

Between eight and nine o'clock the wind tore the iron roof of the Union Passenger Station.

"We all expected death," Morris Sheppard said later, "yet nearly all seemed resigned. Several persons actually slept."

Senator Sheppard died in 1941. His widow, who later married Senator Tom Connally, remembers that "one of Morris' reactions was anger with himself at being caught in such a predicament. He said there were women and children screaming and praying all around him, and some seemed out of their senses."

W. A. Fraser, best man at Sheppard's wedding in 1909, was one of those who had slept.

"Morris said Mr. Fraser became very weary and finally dropped off to sleep," Mrs. Connally recalls, "but he himself did not feel so calm."

Seven blocks away in the Telephone Building, the girl operators were screaming, and Fred Langben suggested something to calm them. He led a group in singing, "My Bonnie Lies Over the Ocean." Before long the telephone operators joined the group in singing other songs.

Those in the Telephone Building were in an east room on the second floor. When the windows there were smashed in, they retreated to another room. Soon they noticed that the weakened walls of steel and plaster were beginning to sway.

"Fred, I think this is the end," Langben's brother said. The two shook hands.

"Don't give up," Fred answered. But he had difficulty heeding his own advice.

Mrs. Vidor and the others in George Boschke's home had been upstairs for quite a while. Earlier, Boschke had ushered them into a bedroom just as the window shutters blew off and glass crashed in.

Then they had gone from room to room. By the time thirty-five of them had crowded into a small room in the rear of the house, many were hysterical.

In the hall were several colored people singing hymns. "We joined in the hymns," Mrs. Vidor recalls. "In the midst of it all I fainted."

The windows were closed tightly, and the room was stuffy. Two men took Mrs. Vidor into another room just as its roof blew off. They brought her back to the packed room and revived her.

Five-year-old King Vidor went to sleep on a wet mattress, but the grownups were not able to sleep—or even rest.

"It sounded like wild animals outside," Mrs. Vidor says. "I thought we were in the Gulf, the way the house was tossed around. We couldn't stand up for long." Outside, swells slapped against the house not far below the upstairs level.

Occasionally someone asked George Boschke about the storm.

"Oh, it's all right," was his stock reply. "Not bad."

"Has the water gone down?"

"No, it hasn't gone down, but it's not bad."

Meanwhile an exhausted Zachary Scott crawled into a linen closet—about 9:00 p.m.—in Saint Mary's Infirmary. As A. J. Beckway had done earlier at the Cotton Exchange, he immediately fell asleep.

But Beckway and his friend, in their room in the downtown building, were awakened by a loud rumble about this time.

"Being youngsters, we didn't know what it was," he remembers. The rumble was Ritter's Saloon and Restaurant collapsing thirty feet away from where they lay. A little later they heard a similar noise; part of another nearby building fell. The boys went back to sleep unaware of what had happened.

When Chief Ketchum heard two hours later that Ritter's had fallen, he hurried there. He helped rescue several persons from the ruins.

By 10:00 P.M. the storm center was well past Galveston, and most of the damage had been done. The wind, now from a southerly direction, was diminishing.

This south wind helped clear the water from the north part of Galveston first, by blowing the water back into the bay. The area to the south, however, was not so fortunate. Here, the wind tended to hold water upon the island, and a line of wrecked houses several blocks inland kept the water from flowing back into the Gulf. Still, most survivors were impressed with the rapidity of the fall of the water that night.

I. H. Kempner had told his coachman earlier to go to the stables, forty feet from the back door of his residence, and release the horses. The man had not returned. Kempner, after waiting about fifteen minutes, tied a rope around his waist, gave the other end of it to a friend on the gallery, and swam in search of the coachman.

He looked without success for "five or ten minutes." Swimming back to the porch, he noticed that the water, which had been ten feet deep in the yard, had receded by at least a foot, and "a bright moon was beginning to show through the clouds." Later the coachman and the horses were found safe on the porch of a nearby house.

Through a hole in the bedroom floor, those in the Cortes residence had been keeping tabs on the height of the water. Henry Cortes, Jr., pushed a long stick into the hole and pulled it out.

"Oh!" he exclaimed. "The water's gone down."

At 10:30 P.M. First Mate Ledden found himself alive and the *Comino* still afloat at her pier. He wrote in the log, "Wharf clear of water."

"The water went down as fast as if a tubful had been turned over," Jim Moore recalls.

When Sarah Littlejohn's father noticed that the water was receding, he immediately went upstairs to give the family the welcome news.

"We went downstairs," Sarah recalled a few days later. "The water was about up to my knees, and the mud and slime were plentiful. We went into the dining room and when we were in there Mamma said she saw something white through the window. We looked and saw it was a white cottage that had drifted there on the side of our house."

The children climbed onto the dining room table and stretched out. Sarah's two sisters went right to sleep, but Sarah could not. A toothache and the wailing of the wind kept her awake.

At about this time the five Clines and the young stranger, who had been pulled out of the water by Joseph, were crawling over debris piled to a height of fifteen feet and higher. They had been carried to within fifty yards of a two-story house, and they headed for it. Joseph went a few feet ahead, and his brother passed the children to him, one at a time. They repeated this process until they reached the house. Then the occupants pulled them in through a second-floor window. Isaac was amazed to discover that they were in his own neighborhood; after drifting for several hours he and the others had floated to a house only several blocks from where his house had been.

Clarence Howth had been cast ashore too. After being carried into the Gulf and back on a window frame, he was stopped by a pile of wreckage. He climbed upon it and lay face down, naked. Shivering and exhausted, be began to cry. He had lost everything in the world except his life.

At Lucas Terrace, a man in the tiny rear bedroom hoisted Daisy Thorne onto the window sill.

"You're the bravest person I've ever known," he said. "I want you to see this first."

She looked out and saw that the water was receding; she could see the tops of the salt cedar trees.

For the people in Miss Thorne's room, this had been a 64-to-1 bet for survival—and they won. For of the sixty-four rooms in Lucas Terrace, only this one was left. Even the room below was a shambles. Water had filled it, and the walls had fallen. The debris packed in there had helped to hold up Miss Thorne's room.

Only one other person in Lucas Terrace lived to tell the tale: a man who had been thrown through a window in the east wing when it fell. He could not even guess how he managed to survive.

The twenty-two people, some of them wondering if anyone else on the whole island could possibly be alive, crawled through a window onto the debris piled outside. They still feared that the rest of the room might fall, even though the storm was abating.

Numb with cold, they waited on the debris for dawn. Daisy Thorne had lost her shoes, and her clothes were soaked. Her long reddish-gold hair, wringing wet, hung straight down over her shoulders; lime and mortar from the fallen walls powdered her hair and stung her skin. She picked up a piece of material she found nearby and draped it around her shoulders. Later she realized that it was part of a carpet.

While Miss Thorne and the others waited for dawn, Walter Bergstrom slept on the stairway in his home, until his father shook him awake.

"Guess it's all over," Walter heard him say.

He rubbed the sleep from his eyes and walked out on the front gallery with his father. In the moonlight they saw a live cow on top of the side of a shed in their yard. The animal was still tethered. They cut the rope, freeing the cow.

Like young Bergstrom, Walter Grover also had slept —sitting on the top steps leading to the second floor of his home. He had chosen a spot near a window because he thought he could help his father, mother, and sister through it if the house fell.

About eleven o'clock Henry Ketchum's mother summoned him.

"Henry, I heard some people call for help in the back yard. Go see what you can do."

On his way out he went through a doorway into the parlor and bumped into something. To his surprise he saw that it was a cow. Several mules, cows, and horses had climbed upon the front gallery, and one cow had wandered into the house through a large window shattered by the wind.

Ketchum saw no one in the yard that night. Returning to the house, he made an observation which he still remembers.

"I'll bet four or five people were drowned in this storm," he said.

About one hour after that, Zachary Scott—in the closet at Saint Mary's Infirmary—awoke and went outside.

"It was as still as death," he recalls.

Actually there was a wind—at midnight it blew from the southeast—but it was nothing compared to what it had been.

After midnight Kate Hermann believed it was safe to open the door of her aunt's house, where the eighteen women were gathered. She looked outside.

"The moon is shining," she told her aunt.

"No," replied Louisa Ahl. "You must be seeing things."

With the door open, they could hear screams coming from the intersection of 19th Street and Avenue N.

About two blocks away, Lucy Klein was calling for help. Ten-year-old Lucy had been on the gallery with the other six members of her family when the house broke up. She was carried so far into the Gulf that she saw no debris around her, except for the box to which she clung. She said later that when night fell it was so black that she could not see her hand when she held it in front of her face. Occasionally the box was swept from her grasp, but she always managed to grab it quickly.

Now Lucy was in the wreckage that all but covered the Charles Schmidt residence; a gate picket had pierced her side. Schmidt's son heard Lucy call, and he brought her into the house. The only medicine available was "a salve used on horses." This was applied to Lucy's wound.

In the early hours of Sunday morning, those who ventured from Port Bolivar Lighthouse saw a bright moon. Then they returned to the lighthousekeeper's residence. Claiborne's daughter, Madge, slept in the crowded house the rest of that night with her back against a wall.

About 3:00 A.M. the Langbens left the Telephone Building to see what had happened to their house. They picked their way over and around the ruins; in one block they saw a mule impaled on an iron fence. They found their house standing, but it was the last one remaining to the east and south, as far as they could see.

At four o'clock two of the policemen who had been with Chief Ketchum constantly—Byrd and Rowan—asked permission to go home. Ketchum granted it.

A short time later, approaching dawn made it possible for Captain Goudge of the *Kendal Castle* to see exactly where his ship was aground: near Texas City, in three feet of water. Captain Page of the *Taunton*, the 2500-ton steamship that had arrived September 6 from Rio de Janeiro, discovered that the water surrounding his vessel at Cedar Point was also only three feet deep.

During the night Goudge had ordered his lifeboats out to rescue people in the water. Later he instructed his crew to erect tents for the homeless, and he shared his ship's food supply with the storm victims. Goudge settled in Galveston after that and, appropriately enough, served twelve years as chairman of the local Red Cross chapter.

In the light of dawn Florence Klaes and her brother, Ralph, who had been swept into the upper branches of adjacent salt cedar trees after Bill Letts' residence broke up, saw that three other persons—also from Letts' house— had been swept into the same grove. The three—Mr. and Mrs. Louis Moore, whose four young daughters had drowned, and a Swedish boy—were in the branches of trees nearby.

The Klaeses, who had grabbed limbs about twenty feet apart during their tumultuous trip through the racing current, had become aware of each other's presence during the night. But clinging to the branches against the wind and the swells, which at times submerged them, had required all their effort. Only after the storm had abated somewhat had Ralph Klaes been able to talk at all.

Now, in the early light of a new day, the Klaeses, like the Moores and the Swedish boy, remained in the tree branches; several feet of water still covered the ground beneath them.

A hysterical shout, coming from somewhere near the grove of trees, startled them.

"Hey! Hey! Hey!" a man yelled. After a brief pause he repeated the exclamation.

"Over here," called Louis Moore.

The pathetic figure of Bill Allen, wading through waist-deep water, came into view. Over a long red-flannel shirt he still wore the collar and tie he had put on Saturday for the housewarming. A hat rested clumsily on his head.

At the sight of him Florence Klaes began laughing, but it was a nervous laugh, a release from the ordeal of the night. The storm had torn every stitch of clothing from her; only a neckband remained.

Bill asked her where Lucy Allen and the rest of his family were.

"I don't know," Florence answered. "Don't you?"

"Why . . . no. I guess they're gone."

Of the six members of the Allen family, Bill was the only one to survive.

The five climbed down from the trees. Ralph Klaes remembers the first thing he saw: the body of a woman bobbing on the surface of the water. It appeared to be caught in a tangle of barbed wire. With her right hand the dead woman clutched the body of a baby girl.

A short time later Ralph found a piece of tarpaulin to wrap around his sister.

The group began wading through the water toward town. Ralph had difficulty walking; his legs had been badly cut by sharp debris during the night.

On the way to town they met a colored man, Will Hodges, with whom the Klaeses were acquainted. Hodges had lost his family. He took off his coat and gave it to Florence, and he joined them on the walk to town.

As the seven passed near Fort Crockett, they saw several bodies of men from Battery O. Some must have been those who had stayed in the barracks; others were soldiers who had left Denver Resurvey School when water was five feet deep on the first floor.

As the group waded up Avenue S, Ralph Klaes fell into a culvert, into water over his head. Hodges pulled him out. After proceeding a short distance farther they found water so deep that they had to detour to the right and walk around Fort Crockett.

On the other side of the city, those who had survived the storm in Daisy Thorne's bedroom were also making their way toward the downtown area. Before they had started—while still awaiting the dawn on a mass of wreckage just outside the bedroom window—Miss Thorne had seen, in the gathering daylight, the body of Mrs. McCauley only a few yards away.

As these twenty-two persons climbed over debris piled two stories high they heard the cries of persons buried beneath them. At first they tried to rescue the trapped victims, but they soon realized it was futile; no human power could save those people. Months were to pass before all the debris could be cleared.

9 SUNDAY AND AFTER

More Pitiable
Than the Dead

SUNDAY MORNING those whose homes had been swept away sought shelter elsewhere—anywhere. The fortunate ones, whose houses had stood, took in the hungry and the homeless, using charcoal furnaces, alcohol stoves, and chafing dishes to heat the food. They brewed coffee—with salt-contaminated water. Hurried, tasteless meals were cooked by people who had these facilities, but for most persons crackers and water—largely brackish—served as breakfast.

As soon as the sun came up, men, women, and children were out looking for their families. They were cut and bruised; many were almost naked. Most streets were so cluttered with debris that it was impossible to walk in them without carefully picking one's way over wreckage of all kinds, and over bodies.

Many of the dead were without clothes. Sharp objects, hurtling through the air, had torn off clothing and mutilated the victims.

Much of Galveston was coated with a foul-smelling slime an inch or so deep; and though the Gulf itself had retreated, pools of water dotted the island.

135

Walter Grover noticed the slime early Sunday morning. "The water was out of the house," he recalls, "but it had left everything covered an inch deep with muck that had the consistency of axle grease. It smelled awful."

The first-floor carpets in Grover's home could not be cleaned and had to be thrown away; the furniture, after much work, was restored, but new upholstery was needed.

After investigating the damage Grover combed the back yard for enough dry wood with which to cook breakfast, but all he could find that would burn were several creosoted blocks that had floated into the yard. The creosote-flavored food nauseated the whole Grover family, and they could barely eat.

At the east end of Galveston Island, Dr. John Mayfield and his two sons discovered that half the quarantine station had been swept away; the rest had been badly damaged.

Early Sunday morning Mayfield observed John Hanson on top of a torpedo casemate, where he had burrowed into the sand and survived the storm. But the undermined casemate tilted at a 45-degree angle, and most of the sand covering it had been washed away. A relatively small patch of sand remained on top; here it was that Hanson had taken refuge. It was quite some time before Dr. Mayfield was successful in coaxing Hanson down from his perch.

On the west side of the city, Walter Bergstrom could see no other house standing between his home and the Gulf, eleven blocks away. The Bergstrom house—built in 1886 in thirty days at a cost of 664 dollars for labor and materials on a 600-dollar lot—was scarcely damaged.

On the mainland, C. A. Paschetag and sixteen others

forced their way out of the overturned boxcar, lying on top of the four-foot embankment. They had to break open the upturned door, which had been locked.

When school superintendent John Hopkins awoke Sunday morning he was startled to see a church steeple in his front yard. He dressed and left for breakfast at the Tremont Hotel. Once outside, he was amazed by the extent of the destruction. On the way downtown Hopkins met a friend and remarked to him that there must have been much loss of life. Even as he talked he became aware of the presence of a child's body floating in a nearby gutter.

Jim Moore also saw a sight that Sunday morning that he would never forget: a horse and a gig, with its driver. The horse was drowned and the man, still on a seat in the gig, was also dead. Later, when the Moores returned to the lot on which their residence had stood, they found only "five or six" gallon jugs of whisky—nothing more. These had been among the groceries Ephraim Moore was delivering.

In the Union Passenger Station downtown, a friend told Jesse Toothaker that Jesse's father was on the first floor inquiring about him. Jesse rushed to greet him.

"I've lost my wife and daughter and the savings of a lifetime," his father said brokenly as they met.

Mr. Toothaker had been holding Jesse's sister, who was ill in bed, when the house fell and knocked her out of his arms. Besides his mother and sister, Jesse lost an uncle and five cousins. All that remained on the lot where his home had been were two salt cedar trees.

In the midst of such tragedy no one thought of holding church services that Sunday morning; most of the church buildings had been destroyed or badly damaged anyway. But Mrs. George Boschke suggested to the guests in her house that they have a prayer meeting. After one person read aloud verses from the Bible, everyone prayed.

On the mainland at Morgan's Point, H. M. Curtin, who had taken the train from Houston to La Porte and walked the rest of the way, also was praying—silently—that he would find his family safe. It seemed hopeless; he had been unable to see any houses at all on Morgan's Point until he squatted and gazed into the distance just above the level of the water through which he waded. He observed then that two of the thirty-five houses there remained; they seemed like dots on the horizon. One belonged to the Coyles, Curtin knew; it was almost in the water. Coming closer, he noticed furniture hanging out of the windows; then, when he reached the house, he was overjoyed to find his family and Randle Pittman, the servant, safe inside.

In Galveston, a nun in Saint Mary's Infirmary asked Zachary Scott to walk down to Saint Mary's Orphanage, about five miles distant, for news of how its occupants had fared. As Scott made his way through littered streets, he passed one vacant lot on which he counted fifteen bodies. When he reached the site of the orphanage he found that only a few scattered bricks remained.

Several days later the bodies of the nuns were found; one still had nine orphans tied to it.

Sunday morning Henry Ketchum looked in his father's yard and counted ten bodies, already twice as many fatalities as he had predicted during the night for all of Galveston.

In the Cotton Exchange Building downtown, A. J. Beckway and his friends were awakened by the father of one of the messenger boys who was in the room. The man had had no idea where his son was and was overjoyed to find him there. The man said that the city east of 13th Street was "swept clean." Actually, this was an understatement, but the boys were astounded by the news. All of Galveston was slow to realize the extent of the disaster.

Shortly after eight o'clock Father James Kirwin, the rector of Saint Mary's Cathedral, began walking over as much of the city as he could reach, and made an estimate: 500 dead. Beckway walked along behind the priest when he made his survey; the youth was appalled at the destruction.

Around 9:00 A.M. men began drifting downtown. At ten o'clock a few of the leading citizens attended a meeting, publicized by word of mouth, in the Tremont Hotel. At that time Mayor Walter C. Jones called another meeting for two o'clock that afternoon to organize a relief committee.

At the morning meeting they discussed the urgency of getting help from the mainland. The group decided to send a party of five to Houston to ask for assistance. One of the few seaworthy craft afloat was W. L. Moody, Sr.'s, steam launch, the *Pherabe;* sometime after ten o'clock the five messengers boarded the vessel, manned by a volunteer crew. As they were leaving, Father Kirwin came to the wharf on his tour of the city.

"Don't exaggerate," the priest advised them. "It's better to underestimate the loss of life. If I were in your place I don't believe I would give it at more than 500."

Shortly after noon the five men scrambled ashore on the mainland at Texas City and walked to La Marque, where they found a railroad handcar on the track and took it to League City. There they met a relief train outbound from Houston, headed toward Galveston. When they had convinced the incredulous crew that it was impossible to get to Galveston by rail, the train returned to Houston, the five messengers with it. They were to arrive in Houston early Monday morning and send appeals for aid to President William McKinley and Governor J. D. Sayers of Texas. But soon they were to discover that James G. Timmins, general superintendent of a Houston compress company, had preceded them. He had been in Galveston during the storm, had left about noon Sunday in a schooner, and had arrived in Houston at eight o'clock Sunday night with the first news of the catastrophe.

Timmins, who had spent Saturday night in the Tremont Hotel, related how the refugees had bemoaned the loss of their relatives and property. All night long they had gathered in groups on stairways and in rooms telling each other of their misfortunes.

Timmins estimated the loss of life as "at least 1000 drowned, killed, or missing," and guessed that 4000 buildings had been destroyed. Thus, the world had its first inkling of the disaster that struck Galveston. First reports are often exaggerated, but this one fell far short.

On Sunday, Galveston turned to collecting its dead. Its citizens had little idea of the scope of the heartbreaking task ahead. Police Chief Ketchum was given the responsibility of supervising the burials.

At a morning roll call that day Ketchum noted that the two policemen, Byrd and Rowan, who had been given permission to go home to see about their families, were back. The chief looked at them questioningly, afraid to ask.

Rowan saluted. "Captain, my wife and children are gone."

"Mine too," Byrd said.

Ketchum was unable to talk. He turned away.

At Union Passenger Station, Morris Sheppard and W. A. Fraser wanted to get back to the mainland quickly. While they were looking for transportation, they came upon an old man wading in bay water some distance away.

Sheppard called to him, asking him to help them get a boat.

"The man turned," Sheppard said, "cursed us with a perfect flood of oaths, walked deliberately out into the bay, and was swept away."

Although many persons wanted to leave the island, two were determined to get there as quickly as they could. They were W. L. Love and Dr. Joe Gilbert.

Love had looked up the foreman of the Houston *Post* composing room and told him he would be absent from work for a few days. He was going to Galveston, he had said, and he did not intend to return until he had found his wife and young son or had convinced himself that they were dead.

He had left Houston when the first news of the disaster began to drift in. He boarded a train headed for Galveston, but washouts forced it to stop eight miles from the bay. Love got off and walked the distance. It took him more than two hours.

Reaching the bay, he could see Galveston Island only two or three miles away. But no boat was in sight, and all that remained of the bridges were lines of piling. Love, looking for anything that would float, spotted a railroad tie near the water's edge. Then he found a coal hook in a nearby locomotive that had been blown off the track. He put the tie in the water and straddled it. With the coal hook he propelled himself along the line of piling. For several hours he worked his way across the bay, half submerged in the water, while a burning sun beat down on the upper half of his body.

He was almost to the island when he saw, floating in the water, the body of a young boy. He looked closely, and suddenly his heart seemed to be in his mouth. Sydney . . . ! As nearly as he could tell, this broken body was his son's. He took the boy in his arms and carried him to a flatcar derailed on the island. Then he went in search of his wife.

He passed scores of bodies, reluctant to look at them closely. He discovered that the whole area around 14th Street and Avenue N, where Mrs. Love had been visiting her mother and grandmother, was swept clean of houses. With a growing feeling of hopelessness, he started for the home of Mrs. Love's cousin, Kate Spann, near the downtown area.

Mrs. Love and her boy were in the house. They had gone there, from Saint Mary's University, after the storm. When Mrs. Love saw her husband walking toward the house, she ran out to meet him, and fainted in his arms.

After a brief reunion Love went back to the flatcar near the bay and buried the body he had thought was his son's.

In Austin, Dr. Joe Gilbert had been horrified when he heard about the storm. He had left immediately for Galveston to find Daisy Thorne—or to learn what had happened to her.

Reaching Houston, Gilbert read news reports listing Daisy Thorne as dead. The man who had been thrown through the window when the east wing of Lucas Terrace collapsed reported everyone in the building lost, including the Thorne family. But then Gilbert ran across Father Kirwin, also in Houston, who had heard that Miss Thorne was alive. The priest passed on to Gilbert this happy news and told him that his fiancée was staying at the home of her uncle, B. G. Tartt, in Galveston. Gilbert hurried on toward the island city.

The looting began Sunday morning. In the afternoon Captain Rafferty collected the remnants of Battery O— twenty-eight men were dead—and guarded the business district; Galveston's regular police force of seventy men was woefully inadequate to cope with the emergency. In a further attempt to keep order in the city Mayor Jones closed the saloons and began swearing in temporary officers.

Later John Blagden, the weather observer on temporary duty in Galveston, was to write his parents in Duluth, Minnesota, describing the conditions.

"The streets are patrolled by armed guards. They are expected to shoot at once anyone found pilfering. I understand four men have been shot today for robbing the dead. I do not know how true it is, for all kinds of rumors are afloat and many of them are false."

Sunday afternoon the search for bodies continued; it was to go on for several months.

Two acquaintances of Lucian Minor, who was last seen attempting to help an aged colored man, were looking for the bodies of their families west of the city when they came across Minor's body. It did not occur to either of them, in their distracted state, to give Minor's friends or relatives this information until several days later. When they did, it was too late to recover the body.

In that area, said Minor's brother, "there were a number of graves where there had been bodies, with no means of identifying Lucian's. While we know he was buried, we will never know in what grave."

About sundown that same day E. F. Gerloff finally freed himself from the capsized boat, which had trapped him when it overturned the evening before. Gerloff heard the boat strike ground, and he dived under the water, escaping—with no little difficulty—through a hatch. Once outside, he heard someone mumbling inside the boat. He went back in and pulled out his father; Gerloff, who had spent hours fighting to keep his head above water while the swells tossed the overturned boat like a cork, had not known that his father was trapped in the boat too.

The dazed pair wondered where they had landed. They were certain it was either Cuba or Mexico. Actually they were near Virginia Point. One of the first sights they saw was the *Roma* aground near where the bridges from the mainland to Galveston Island had stood.

On Monday recovery of the bodies began in earnest. Little had been accomplished Sunday; the city had been too demoralized, and there had been too much else to do first. Some of Galveston's leading citizens joined in the ghastly work, hoping to influence others to volunteer. Four morgues were set up, but they soon became inadequate.

A quick way of disposal was obviously required, and two city aldermen proposed burial at sea. A barge was brought to the 12th Street wharf; firemen took the bodies there on their wagons.

When few men volunteered for the job of handling the dead, troops and temporary officers put men to work at gun point. But the longer they worked the more bodies they found.

"It soon became so that the men could not handle those bodies without stimulants," Father James Kirwin said. "I am a strong temperance man. I pledge the children to total abstinence at communion, but I went to the men who were handling those bodies, and I gave them whisky."

Young Henry Ketchum saw the laborers drinking, at intervals, during this work.

"There was a barrel of whisky, with tin cups, in the barge," Ketchum recalls. "Every time a worker made a trip down into the barge he took a drink."

By Monday night 700 bodies were on the barge. Hope of identifying most of them had been abandoned. That would have required too much time; moreover, many bodies were beyond recognition. A new crew was impressed to bury the dead at sea late Monday night, and the barge was towed into the Gulf. The bodies were to be weighted and consigned to the depths.

But scores of bodies reappeared on the beach the very next morning. Some were weighted; many were not. The impressed men had wanted to get the job done quickly.

Burial at sea was abandoned after that. Carrying bodies through the streets on open wagons to the wharf was too demoralizing and unsafe anyway. From Tuesday on, Galveston disposed of its dead as it found them. Sometimes this was by burial in shallow graves, more frequently by cremation. Many were burned in the debris where they were found.

The city was to spend months in this work. On October 29, almost two months after the storm, laborers cleaning wreckage from the streets found ten more bodies, and others were found even after that. Some were not discovered until years later, when skeletons were occasionally uncovered in the sand on mainland beaches.

On October 2 workers extricated the bodies of two boys from the wreckage. They were identified as Scott Mc-Cluskey, twelve, and Earl McCluskey, four, sons of Charles McCluskey. Earl was clasped tightly in the right arm of his brother, whose left arm was badly torn. Evidently Scott had ignored a painful injury to protect the younger boy as long as he was able.

Their father had been on the *Comstock* during the storm.

"I have lost four—my wife and three children," the sorrowful man said when he was informed that his boys had been found. "It has been an awful blow to me, but I'm proud that Scott died a hero's death. He was manly, upright, lovable—and as brave as a boy can be."

A little after dark the next day the body of Isaac Cline's wife was also found, her ring and other jewelry helping in the identification. Mrs. Cline's body was recovered from debris at 28th Street and Avenue P; it was under the very wreckage on which Isaac Cline, his brother, three daughters, and the young stranger had drifted until it went aground there.

But this was not to occur until almost a month after the cleanup began. On the Monday following the storm, while the bodies were being taken to the barge, an Associated Press story carried this lead:

"The city of Galveston is wrapped in sackcloth and ashes. She sits beside her unnumbered dead and refuses to be comforted. Her sorrow and suffering are beyond description. Her grief is unspeakable."

On this same day President McKinley acknowledged the appeal telegraphed to him by the five messengers from Galveston. The President wired Governor Sayers of Texas:

"The reports of the great calamity which has befallen Galveston and other points on the coast of Texas excite my profound sympathy for the sufferers as they will stir the hearts of the whole country. Whatever help it is possible to give shall be promptly extended. Have directed the secretary of war to supply rations and tents upon your request. William McKinley."

Andrew Carnegie was another early contributor; he sent 20,000 dollars. Standard Oil gave 10,000 dollars. Sir Thomas Lipton, the tea magnate, cabled from London an order that his New York office give 1000 dollars. Johnstown, Pennsylvania, began collecting donations without being asked; its area in 1889 had lost 2200 persons in a flood.

Messages of sympathy poured in from all over the world, including condolences from the president of France, the king of Italy, Kaiser Wilhelm of Germany, and many others.

On Monday, while the world was discovering the extent of the disaster at Galveston, Dr. Joe Gilbert boarded a train in Houston headed toward the island city. He met a friend, Dr. Edward Randall, Sr., a Galveston physician who also lectured at the University of Texas Medical College in the city.

Randall and his wife and son were returning from a trip abroad. They had been on a train near Saint Louis when they heard about the storm; when they reached Houston, Randall had left his family in that city and hurried on toward Galveston. He carried what he thought were his medical instruments, but after a while he realized it was his son's toy train, in a similar bag. He asked Gilbert to hold his medical kit for him. Then, settled in the chair car, Randall and Gilbert began a lengthy conversation. Randall asked his friend what he planned to do in Galveston.

"Find Daisy and marry her," Gilbert answered.

Other talk followed. Several minutes passed, and Dr. Gilbert curiously eyed the bag he was holding in his lap. It seemed to him rather heavy for medical instruments.

"What is this?" Gilbert asked.

"Just carry it," Randall answered. "It's valuable." Dr. Randall later had his instruments sent to Galveston.

Gilbert reached B. G. Tartt's grocery store Monday evening. With him by then was an uncle of Miss Thorne whom Gilbert had encountered after reaching Galveston. The store was closed, but the people living upstairs told the two men that Daisy Thorne was staying at the Tartt residence. They reached the house late Monday night.

Tuesday morning Charles Vidor was finally reunited with his wife and son at the Boschke residence. Vidor told them he had spent the night of the storm on rafters at the bagging company; he had been unable to reach them sooner because many of the debris-littered streets were impassable.

That Tuesday morning George Boschke obtained a Southern Pacific boat for himself and his family, and he asked Mrs. Vidor if she would like to come with them to the mainland. Vidor insisted that she and King leave the city for a while. The two boys from Fort Worth and Mrs. Vidor's cousin also went.

Crossing the bay, they saw that it was littered with wreckage and hundreds of bodies. After they reached the mainland, they climbed into a boxcar and rode a train into

Houston. There they were mobbed by people wanting news of relatives.

Mrs. Vidor remembers laughing for the first time since the storm. In the excited throng was a man who must have just finished dinner; he had a long, white beard, and out of the beard hung a toothpick.

"It bobbed up and down when he talked," Mrs. Vidor recalls.

Later she and King went to Dallas to stay with a sister. Arriving there, she and her son entered a hack—and Mrs. Vidor realized that she could not remember her sister's address, although she had written to her frequently. Only the name of the street on which her sister lived came to her mind.

The hack driver was patient, knowing that his fare had just arrived from Galveston. He said, "Oh, that's all right; you've been through a lot." He drove up and down the street until Mrs. Vidor finally recognized the house.

On the same Tuesday that Mrs. Vidor and her son left Galveston, Mayor Jones dispatched a second appeal for help "to the people of the United States."

"It is my opinion, based on personal information, that 5000 people have lost their lives here," the mayor stated. "Approximately one-third of the residence portion of the city has been swept away. There are several thousand people who are homeless and destitute; how many, there is no way of finding out. Arrangements are now being made to have the women and children sent to Houston and other places, but the means of transportation are limited. Thousands are still to be cared for here. We appeal to you for immediate aid."

Publisher William Randolph Hearst had already determined to be of assistance. On the same day that Mayor

Jones made his second appeal, Hearst advised Governor Sayers by telegram that the first of several relief trains to be sent to Galveston would leave that night.

In charge of one relief train, which represented Hearst's Chicago *American,* was Dr. William L. Crosthwait, a Texan. He had been in Chicago when he heard newsboys shouting the news of the storm. He went to the Chicago *American* building for more information and struck up a conversation with a Hearst aide. The publisher himself walked past just then, and the aide introduced the doctor from Texas. Hearst invited Crosthwait into his office and inquired if he would be willing to take charge of a relief train for Galveston.

Crosthwait would. Hearst wrote a check for 50,000 dollars for expenses and told his secretary to have it cashed.

On Wednesday the center of the storm that struck Galveston disappeared into the North Atlantic area, passing north of Halifax. From Texas it had traveled into Oklahoma and Kansas, where it had turned northeastward. Later it had crossed over the Great Lakes and part of Canada.

At the time the storm was leaving land, a rumor was spreading through Galveston that a hurricane even worse than Saturday's was expected to strike the city. A *News* reporter hurried to the Weather Bureau office for verification. He was informed that there was no truth to the story.

On this day Charles D. Anderson, Jr., was finally reunited with his parents at Fort Point Lighthouse. Dr. John Mayfield, the quarantine officer, took him from town to the jetty in a boat, and young Anderson swam from the jetty to the lighthouse.

On Thursday, September 13, martial law was declared,

although the city had been under similar restrictions since the day after the storm. Martial law was to last until noon, September 21.

Albert E. Smith, one of the earliest newsreel photographers, arrived in Galveston about this time with his camera. (Some of his motion pictures of the Boer War had been shown in Galveston—at the Olympia—on the night of September 2, just six days before the storm.) Smith had great difficulty reaching Galveston; a permit was required for travel from Houston to the island city. Although Smith carried letters from Thomas A. Edison and Mayor Van Wyck of New York explaining the importance of his trip, he found one hard to obtain.

"I'm afraid, young man, you will have to wait," the official had said.

"It's important . . ."

"We already have more people in there than we can feed, and we are letting in no one at the present time. See me later."

"When?"

"In about a week."

Protests had been unsuccessful. Then Smith remembered a card given him by a man he had met on the train. The man, a Mr. Chittenden, represented a New York wrecking company. The firm's specialty was ships.

Smith went to another official, gave him the card, and said he would like to see about getting those big ships, which were aground, afloat. He was given the permit.

Landing at Galveston, Smith and his motion-picture equipment were spotted by Texas guardsmen. Photographers were unpopular on the island; too many concentrated on taking pictures of nude bodies. By way of punishment some had been put to work removing corpses.

"There's one of those photographers," growled a guardsman. He poked the end of a bayonet against Smith's stomach.

"He's not a photographer; he's a surveyor," said a reporter who had come over with Smith. The soldier let him pass, and Smith breathed a profound sigh of relief.

Before Smith departed from the island—after shooting many feet of film—he saw one sight he was never to forget.

"A man had been caught cutting fingers from bodies to get the rings," Smith recalls. "He had his pockets full. The soldiers pulled a sugar sack over his head, stood him up, and shot him."

Besides Smith, other persons had also hurried to Galveston after the storm. One of them was Clara Barton, president of the American Red Cross, who came to offer help. Another was Joel Chandler Harris, known for his Uncle Remus stories, who came to report the storm. Harris summed up the situation perhaps better than anyone else.

"The condition of thousands of those who have been spared is far more pitiable than that of the dead," he wrote. "Their resources have been swept away by wind and tide, and they are desolate in the midst of desolation."

Few families survived without the loss of at least one member, and in some cases whole families were lost: R. H. Peek, the city engineer who had been interviewed about streets by a Galveston *News* reporter the day before the storm, was drowned, along with his wife and six children. Peek had tied his family together with a long rope; he probably thought he could save them if the house fell. But when it collapsed all eight members of the family were drowned together.

No one escaped without losing some property. A few

buildings, like the one still occupied by the Galveston *Daily News*, were relatively undamaged, but this was the exception. Isaac Cline's official report to the Weather Bureau told the story.

"Where 20,000 people lived on the eighth not a house remained on the ninth, and who occupied the houses may, in many instances, never be known."

A. G. Youens, Galveston insurance inspector, estimated that 3636 residences were demolished. Youens had survived the collapse of his house witnessed by his neighbor, S. O. Young, but lost two children—a daughter, Lily, and a son, George.

Various estimates were made concerning the amount of property damage, but the totals are meaningless today. The best idea of financial loss comes from these figures: the city's total assessment then was about 28,000,000 dollars. Of this, 15,000,000 dollars in property was swept away. Up to 300 feet of shoreline, totaling 1500 acres, was swallowed by the Gulf, and some of this land loss never has been recovered. (The insurance companies, however, did not pay out so much as might be imagined; Galveston then had relatively little coverage.)

The first wedding in Galveston after the storm took place Thursday, September 13, when Dr. Joe Gilbert married Miss Daisy Thorne. They were wed in Grace Episcopal Church. Mud was caked several inches deep in the aisle.

"Nobody thought of cleaning up the mud," Daisy Thorne Gilbert remembers now. "They couldn't even get the bodies removed from the wreckage which covered much of the city."

The bride wore a white shirtwaist, borrowed from a

friend, and a black skirt she bought after the storm; the skirt had been soaked during the overflow. She also wore a white felt hat, "on which something pink had faded."

Dr. Gilbert wore a business suit. When he left Austin —fearing Daisy Thorne might be dead—he had certainly not thought to bring a wardrobe for a wedding.

That night the couple stayed at the B. G. Tartt residence. Daisy's relatives wanted to move the newlyweds into a room of their own, but the Gilberts would not think of it; they knew it would have caused some of the others to double up, and the house was already crowded. The bride slept with her mother, and Dr. Gilbert slept in another room.

When the two left for Austin the next day, Mrs. Gilbert carried with her one of her five pet cats. It had survived the storm by climbing into the top drawer of the wardrobe in her room. The other four were victims of the angry Gulf.

10

A Dream That Was

FIFTY-SIX YEARS after the storm Mrs. Charles Vidor—by then a resident of Los Angeles, California—was to make a comment that expressed the affection for the city felt by most nineteenth-century Galvestonians.

"It was just a pile of sand, but I loved it. So many wonderful things happened to me there."

The city is still a delightful place, but many old-timers will tell you that it never has been the same since the storm. September 8, 1900, proved to be the end of the nineteenth century for Galveston, and it is a date that no one who was in the city then can ever forget.

It will always remain vivid in Mrs. W. L. Love's memory. Three weeks after the storm, after she had returned to Houston, she read a newspaper story describing bodies found by the street gangs the day before. Two rings had been taken off one body, the item reported. Engraved inside one were the word "Mispah" and a date of July 22, 1855. Immediately Mrs. Love realized that it was her mother's wedding ring, and she left by train for Galveston. There, with her brother, Will, she went to the custodian's office, where items that had been found were tagged with the finder's name.

155

Mrs. Love hoped to discover the name of the person who had found her mother's body. Politely she asked a man in the office to let her see the rings. He refused.

"I have a list here of some of my mother's things," she then said. "Will you let me see if anything you have compares with it?"

"No," the man answered. Perhaps he was merely being cautious; a number of persons had dishonestly claimed articles after seeing them.

"Why, you are a hardhearted wretch," Mrs. Love exclaimed. "I'm trying to locate my mother's body!"

Her brother tried to ease the tension.

"She's upset," he said. "Otherwise she'd know you can't show these things to her."

A friend of Mrs. Love's brother overheard the conversation. He immediately joined the group.

"Will, come with me to the safe," he said, "and I'll give you the two rings—and a watch and goblet. They have your mother's name on them."

From the tags on the rings Mrs. Love and her brother learned the name of the man who found their mother's body; he was a street-gang foreman. He told them that the body was buried between two small cottages near the northwest corner of 19th Street and Avenue N, where it had been found. Will saw that it was removed to Galveston Cemetery.

The sad months that followed the storm still haunt Mrs. Charles Vidor.

"All winter long you never saw such a place," she recalls. "Most people were in mourning, and everybody was sad. Galveston was a ruined city."

In an attempt to make their own existence endurable that winter, the Vidors and Boschkes and a few other friends met every Sunday night for supper. Invariably they would gather around the piano and sing, and always they would get around to singing a recently written song, "The Galveston Storm."

"We would cry," Mrs. Vidor remembers. ". . . Cry so much we couldn't sing."

Many left the city permanently during this period. Many thought that rebuilding was impossible. But W. L. Moody, Sr., who had been in New York when the storm struck, told his son, "If they do abandon the city, remember: the fewer the people the better the fishing." Moody's son stayed in Galveston, and as the years passed he enjoyed much success in several business ventures. In 1954, when he died, he was one of the wealthiest men in the United States.

Galveston made an amazing recovery from the disaster.

On Wednesday, September 12—four days after the storm—Pabst and Leinbach, wholesale grocers, displayed merchandise for sale. Although many of the canned goods had lost their labels, the goods sold quickly.

That same day the city received its first mail. But because the streets were piled high with debris and because several carriers were dead, delivery was impossible; residents were asked to come to the post office instead.

On Wednesday, too, water was turned into the city's mains. It was several days, however, before it reached more than a few houses.

On Thursday, September 13, the Galveston *Daily News* printed a full-sized paper. From Sunday through Wednesday it had issued only small editions, printed on a hand press.

That day the telegraph was back in operation. The first

message, sent at 4:16 P.M., was followed by hundreds of others, from Galvestonians to out-of-town friends and relatives.

On Friday, September 14, the banks opened. The first real estate transaction took place when one citizen bought a lot and house for 3000 dollars.

On Saturday—one week after the storm—mule cars began running on some streets. This was an occasion for joy; it caused almost as much excitement as the first electric car. No. 66, pulled by a mule named Lazy Lil, made three trips during the afternoon—from Market to 21st to Broadway to 40th and back. The track was covered with grass and mud, and Lazy Lil was exhausted at the completion of the last trip.

That same Saturday a few streets and stores were electrically lighted.

On Sunday, September 16, some churches held services. Only four church buildings in the entire city were relatively undamaged, and few others were in any condition to accommodate a crowd. The First Church of Christ Scientist extended the use of its building to other congregations. Its own eleven o'clock service, however, hinged on the weather.

"In case of rain it will be impossible to hold services," stated a church announcement, "because many windows are out and the roof is damaged."

On Monday, September 17, long-distance telephone service was re-established.

A railroad bridge across the bay was rebuilt in five working days. It was completed at 3:00 A.M., Friday, September 21, and the first train—Santa Fe's—arrived in Galveston at 6:20 A.M.

Schools opened October 22. Superintendent John W.

Hopkins directed a public subscription campaign which raised 80,000 dollars to restore them. New York City school children alone gave 27,907 dollars of that amount.

The rapid reconstruction prompted Thomas Scurry, adjutant general of Texas and commander of Galveston during the period of martial law, to observe: "I do not think I exaggerate when I say that at no time in all history have there been examples of nobler loyalty or more heroic determination. The credit for what has been done belongs in an overwhelmingly large measure to the brave people of this city."

The storm made at least three permanent changes in the city, and all were beneficial.

Galveston had talked of building a sea wall before the tragedy. General Braxton Bragg had recommended a system of protective works as early as 1874. At that time, however, it was considered too expensive. Besides, the city had withstood other storms and evidently did not need one.

But on Sunday morning, September 9, Galveston citizens realized the value of having such a wall. A high barrier of debris had formed between the area of total destruction and the rest of the city. This debris, acting more or less as a breakwater, had been largely responsible for preventing even more damage.

The sea-wall contract was let September 19, 1902, for 1,198,318 dollars. (The actual cost was almost half a million more than that figure.) The sea wall was to stretch for six miles along the Gulf side of the city and be built of reinforced concrete on creosoted piling driven forty feet into the sand. In front of the wall would be a protective layer of granite blocks extending twenty-seven feet toward the sea. The wall itself was to be sixteen feet thick at the base and stand seventeen feet above the mean low tide—more than a foot above the 1900 storm tide.

It was completed July 29, 1904, and proved its value in a 1915 tropical hurricane, which brought a fourteen-foot tide and twenty-one-foot waves. Property damage was cut to 4,500,000 dollars, and only twelve lives were lost. Since that time the sea wall has been extended even more.

During the storm it had also become obvious that Galveston was too low. Some daring citizens, risking being laughed at as proposing the impossible, now suggested raising the level of the city by pumping sand from the floor of the Gulf onto the island. But that would require raising nearly every building in the area that had to be filled, and some of them were large brick structures.

Only two bids for this work were received, and one of them proposed raising just the grades of the streets—not of private property. The other bid (2,080,175 dollars) suggested using self-propelled hopper dredges to be operated on a canal, which would be dug through the city. Fourteen million cubic yards of fill would be dredged into the area.

E. R. Cheesborough, a leader in reconstruction, still remembers a comment made by Congressman Walter Gresham before the project was publicized: "The people are going to lynch us when they find out about this canal." Surprisingly, Gresham was wrong.

A grade-raising board, aided by Galveston real estate dealers, agreed to furnish the right of way for the canal, and not a single condemnation suit was required. Citizens who lived along the proposed route of the canal voluntarily consented to having their houses moved to vacant lots. Later, when the canal had served its purpose, it was filled, and these houses were moved back. Taxes were paid by the grade-raising board during this period; the stricken city could do nothing more.

Raising the grade required raising 2146 buildings before the filling was begun. Streetcar tracks, fire plugs, and water pipes also had to be raised. Trees, shrubs, and flowers had to be removed if the owner wanted to save them. The largest building raised was a 3000-ton church. It was boosted off the ground (with jacks) five feet; then fill was pumped underneath. Services were not interrupted.

The canal, begun in July, 1904, cut through the heart of the residential district; it was two and one-half miles long, 300 feet wide, twenty feet deep. Sand, sucked up from the bottom of the Gulf, was brought in through the canal by the hopper dredges and discharged through pipelines into defined areas. The water emitted with the sand drained back into the canal. The grade was thus raised to a height of almost seventeen feet near the sea wall; it sloped gradually downward from there to the north.

The first grade raising was completed in 1910, and the canal was filled. Galveston then was as safe from hurricanes as it could be.

Finally, as a result of the storm, it was obvious that Galveston's form of city government had to be changed. Before the storm Galveston had elected a mayor and twelve aldermen, one from each of twelve wards. This had long been an unsatisfactory and cumbersome system. The budget usually exceeded the income, and on the morning of September 8, 1900, the city was virtually bankrupt. Changes now were not only desirable; they were a necessity.

A forerunner of the new government was the Central Relief Committee, hurriedly set up in the Tremont Hotel that Sunday afternoon after the storm. This committee was composed of men appointed to different duties: distributing relief supplies, burying the dead, handling city funds, caring for the injured, assuring proper law enforcement, and handling city correspondence. The responsibility for each duty was specifically one person's. Later, when the state granted Galveston's request for a new charter based on this plan, the city commission form of government was born. (It soon spread across the United States.) Galveston had a commission of five members, one of whom was mayor. All of them were elected at large every two years. To each commissioner fell the sole responsibility for running one department; he alone was to blame if anything went wrong in it.

September 8, 1900, is still a date the city would like to forget. It does not boast of its experience with the storm that almost destroyed it. (Until recently a merchant had the high-water mark of that fateful night showing on his building, but so many persons told him it did not look good for the city that he obliterated it, after all these years.)

One reason for Galveston's reluctance to publicize the tragedy is the fear of frightening away people, both tourists and residents. But a massive sea wall and tireless grade raising, which still continues, make Galveston one of the best protected cities on any coast.

Another reason is that the horror of that night still lives in the memories of its survivors. Some do not want to talk about it at all; others do, but reluctantly. And, of course, many talk freely of their experiences in the storm. Life for most survivors was never quite the same afterward, and months were required for many to return to even a semblance of normal living.

Daisy Thorne Gilbert made the adjustment more swiftly than most others, but her husband told her that for several weeks after the couple moved to Austin she frequently twitched nervously in her sleep. Yet, characteristically, she displayed none of this nervousness while awake. (Mrs. Gilbert, of English stock, is fond of borrowing an old saying to point out that "English people have a great faculty for flying into a calm.") It was no surprise to a friend that Daisy was able to write this tranquil sentence in a letter only a few days after the storm:

"I feel that I have been given a marvelous blessing," she observed, "to have been brought so close to the infinite and to see how small finite things are."

Isaac Cline, too, displayed exceptional resilience of character after the storm. Despite the tragic death of his wife, he was back on duty at the Weather Bureau office on Sunday. From Monday, September 10, through Sunday, September 16, however, he was absent from the office—belatedly hospitalized with injuries suffered that Saturday night. But as soon as he was able to do so, he prepared and mailed his special report to the U. S. Weather Bureau. Cline later gave up his recreational study of medical climatology to concentrate on tropical cyclones; he contributed a vast amount of information toward the understanding of them.

Joseph Cline, like his brother, required hospitalization after the storm. But he, too, postponed it as long as possible. A yellowing page in the daily journal for September, 1900—still kept in the Galveston Weather Bureau office —attests to this.

"I. M. Cline absent today," it notes for September 10,

"on account of injuries received in the storm. J. L. Cline left in charge. Unable to do much."

In 1955 the two brothers died eight days apart during one of the worst hurricane seasons the United States has ever experienced, although the death toll for that entire period was a mere fraction of Galveston's loss in the 1900 storm. Isaac Cline succumbed in New Orleans at 8:30 P.M. August 3, at the age of ninety-three; at the moment he died, Hurricane Connie was gaining strength 850 miles east of Puerto Rico. Joseph Cline died in a Texas hospital on August 11, at the age of eighty-four; that very night Hurricane Connie hit the North Carolina coast, causing tides eight feet above normal and flooding Carolina Beach. After Connie, the warnings went up for Diane, which proved to be the nation's first billion-dollar hurricane.

Like the Clines, Police Chief Ed Ketchum was a public servant, and during his term of office he always felt that duty should come first. He remained at police headquarters for thirty-six hours after the storm before going home. On September 30, however, Ketchum resigned—after fifteen months as police chief—to attempt to rebuild his own general contracting business.

Of several hundred horses and mules in his father's stables, only "25 or 30" were ever recovered, Henry Ketchum recalls. When Ed Ketchum died some thirty years later most of the leading citizens of Galveston came to the funeral, paying their last respects to the Yankee who had won acclaim, even among Confederates.

Ephraim Moore's residence ten blocks from the Ketchums had disappeared during the storm, but he also readjusted quickly; his self-reliance proved to be a distinct advantage. Moore was able to provide for his family: he moved them into a house that had floated to the intersection of 33rd Street and Avenue M. There they stayed, with no furniture, for three or four days, sleeping on the floor. Then they moved into another vacant house, and equipped it with furniture found in the debris. Later Moore bought a house that had remained intact, although it had floated off its foundation, and he moved it to his lot.

Jim Moore still lives in this house—his father died years ago—but he is no longer the trusting, thirteen-year-old, freckled-faced youngster he was then. "If they say a storm's coming now," he declares, "I get to a safe place."

No striking change was discernible in Walter Grover after the storm. In fact, he will tell you even today, "Under similar conditions I suppose I would do now what I did then." Grover, whose insatiable curiosity led him to walk through the storm that Saturday until its violence almost cost him his life, still loves the Gulf of Mexico.

"I have never had enough of it," he says, after living beside it constantly since 1869, the year he was born. Today he still enjoys walking along the beach, collecting shells.

Many other survivors are not so forgiving toward the Gulf.

Ralph Klaes, who could not swim that Saturday night when he was swept into the top branches of a salt cedar tree, still cannot swim, although he enjoys boating on Galveston Bay.

"I don't care anything about that water—for swimming," he observes. "I had enough of it that night."

If you talk about the storm with E. F. Gerloff, who was trapped in the sailboat after it had capsized with him and his family, he will make an even stronger statement: "The storm took the life out of you. It's always on your mind. No matter what you do, where you are—it's there."

Two weeks to the day after the storm ravaged Galveston, attorney Clarence Howth made a pilgrimage. For the first time since that dreadful Saturday, he walked out to the lot on which his house had stood, near the beach.

A garden hose still attached to the water faucet marked the site. He had left the hose there on the evening of the seventh, after watering his young cauliflower plants in the back yard.

"It seemed as a dream," Howth said, "of a thing that had never been."

Acknowledgments

NOBODY KNOWS the complete story of what happened at Galveston; nobody ever will know.

How many lives were lost is an unanswerable question. Death estimates ranged from 3000 to 12,000 and even higher, depending on the personalities and interests of those making the guesses. A partial list of the dead compiled by the Galveston *News* after the storm had more than 4200 names. Hundreds more were never identified.

The best estimate and the one accepted by most people is that 6000 lost their lives in Galveston and possibly as many as 2000 died in other coastal areas that night. Morrison and Fourmey, publishers of the *Galveston City Directory*, are among those who give this figure for the city's loss. Their canvass of Galveston in 1901 lends authority to the estimate.

Nobody knows, even today, exactly how this or any other hurricane originated; Gordon E. Dunn, meteorologist in charge of the Miami Weather Bureau office (who is often referred to as the world's foremost hurricane forecaster), is among those who subscribe to this statement.

Nobody knows exactly where the storm was formed or the path it took during its first few days of life. In 1900 hurricane reports were fragmentary. Stephen Lichtblau, meteorologist in charge of the New Orleans Weather Bureau office, states that records in his office show that the storm might have had its in-

167

ception August 26, "apparently a short distance west of Dakar." Mr. Lichtblau points out that there were several storms in progress during that September, however, and this might not be the one that hit Galveston. The track of the storm, as charted in issues of the *Monthly Weather Review* for 1900, was used in this book.

(Mr. Dunn and Mr. Lichtblau read certain parts of the manuscript, especially the passages relative to characteristics of tropical hurricanes in general.)

Nobody can realize the horror of that night unless he lived it. Survivors are unanimous in stating this.

In a letter written a few days after the storm to Miss Anna Howard, another teacher at Rosenberg School (who was out of town), Daisy Thorne Gilbert said:

"The horror of that time I can never describe. But there was no frenzied fear among us. All were desperately calm and quiet except for prayers. Each one felt he was almost face to face with his Maker.

"Death, and an awful death, seemed inevitable.

"If you could have looked out on that awful water rolling in as high as small hills—turning a piano or a big porcelain bathtub over and over like a little bobbing cork—you would have thought nothing could have stayed on the island. All that water rushed by us.

"A mountain of water would come rolling toward us and we would shudder, thinking our little room couldn't stand another shock. Walls would creak and groan; the wind shrieked. We could hear nothing else. All would give up. Then the wave would roll on, and our little room still stood."

(Daisy Thorne Gilbert proved to be an ideal wife for a doctor. For nearly half a century after her marriage she visited many patients with Dr. Gilbert on his evening rounds. Thousands of ex-students of the University of Texas will remember, as I do, the late "Dr. Joe"; for twenty-seven years he gave most of the physical examinations to entering freshmen, and he cared for many students when they became ill.)

There is still a question of when the wind gauge blew away

that Saturday. Most 1900 reporters said 6:15 P.M., the time given by Isaac Cline in his official report to the U. S. Weather Bureau. But a paragraph in the *Monthly Weather Review* of September, 1900, in which Cline's report appeared, stated: "Attention is called to the fact that the clocks and self-registers at regular weather bureau stations are all set to 75th meridian —or Eastern Standard—time; as far as practicable, only this standard of time is used in the text of the *Review*, since all weather bureau observations are required to be taken and recorded by it." (Galveston was, and is, a regular Weather Bureau station.)

Another fact bears out the assumption that the wind gauge blew away at 5:15, not 6:15, P.M. The Galveston Weather Bureau office still retains the original records of eight o'clock morning and evening readings for that period. These were specifically labeled then as having been taken at eight o'clock, 75th meridian time; this was seven o'clock in Galveston. In the original record of 8:00 P.M. readings for Saturday, September 8, 1900, there is a space for maximum wind velocity since the last reading—which was at 8:00 A.M., 75th meridian time.

In that space is the figure "84"—miles an hour—and this note: "for 10 hours and 15 minutes." Ten hours and fifteen minutes from 8:00 A.M. (75th) would be 6:15 P.M. (75th) or 5:15 P.M. Galveston time.

In piecing together the story of the storm I have avoided as much as possible using previously published narratives and secondhand accounts. Original records, when available, have been relied on, as have first-person experience stories. Files of the Galveston *Daily News* (commonly known then and now simply as the *News*), which seemed to give the best and most accurate coverage of the storm of any newspaper, also were used extensively. Much information was gleaned from personal interviews with survivors themselves.

Fifty-six years, however, is a long time. Memory, even of this catastrophe, fades. Some survivors tell the same story with a few differences—in times, names, distances, and so on. These facts have been verified when possible. When this has not been possible, the most logical account was used. (Most survivors said the Weather Bureau office then was in the Trust Building, but a check of the original records in the Galveston office showed that it was in the Levy Building; it was moved into that building June 25, 1898, and moved out, to the Trust Building, November 27, 1900.)

But survivors recall an amazing amount of detail about their own experiences in the storm, considering that more than half a century has gone by since that terrible night. Most of them—like Bill Simpson, who rode out the storm on the two-masted schooner *Hard Times* while steamers were being swept aground—supplied every possible detail, and it was obvious that they strove for accuracy.

Bill Simpson—his brother, Jess, died several years ago—patiently related in detail how he and his brother handled the boat to keep it afloat. Jess stayed at the tiller; Bill handled the sails.

Was any great difficulty experienced in handling the boat? Mr. Simpson was asked.

"We both were sailboat men from childhood," Mr. Simpson replied, "and the boat—and sails—were not too difficult to handle; it had to be done just one way. That, of course, was the right way, under the conditions that existed at that time.

"My brother was captain, and he was at the tiller. The wind was blowing so hard and making so much noise that he couldn't shout orders to me. All he could do was point to what he wanted done. But I knew as well as he what to do with the sails anyway."

Mr. Simpson then went on to relate what he did with the sails during the trip from Pier 19, in town, to the area north of Pelican Island where the *Hard Times* finally anchored. He described this with no hesitation, an indication of how indelibly it is fixed in his memory.

But Mr. Simpson, too, was conscious of an inability to describe the night. "Just don't let anybody tell you," he finally suggested, "that it wasn't one hell of a storm."

Survivors differ on the storm wave, among other things. Some say there was none. Possibly the wall of debris between

these people and the Gulf made the sudden rise less percep-
tible. But there was a storm wave of four feet; this is mentioned in Isaac Cline's official report.

Henry Ketchum remembers that there were no large waves
or swells hitting his house; the water was relatively flat. The
dam of wrecked buildings, however, was between his house
and the Gulf.

Stories also say that people became insane or gray-haired
overnight. These evidently are untruths. The rebuilding of the
city immediately after the storm offered proof of how level-
headed its citizens were.

Stories of looting were exaggerated, but there was some of
this. Albert Smith saw one case. There probably would be
looting anywhere, in such a catastrophe. Fingers with rings
were cut off bodies, and people were caught and shot on the
spot for doing this.

Generally, however, the people of Galveston reacted admir-
ably. In modern history few other cities of comparable size
have, in time of peace, been called upon to do what Galvestonians did: virtually rebuild a destroyed city. Today's Galveston is a tribute to their courageous work.

Several organizations have helped with this book. Baylor
University, which Isaac Cline's wife attended, is one. The oldest university in the state, Baylor has much historical material
in its main library and in its Texas Collection.

The Corps of Engineers, Galveston district, made available
information through G. J. Micheletti, chief of its technical
liaison branch.

The Galveston *News-Tribune*—the *News* is Texas' oldest
newspaper—helped, as did the Rosenberg Library in that city.
Bill Holman, librarian, has on hand the state's third most ex-
tensive historical collection. The letters of John Blagden, Sarah
Littlejohn, and the Sealy Hospital nurse (whose name is not
known) are in the Rosenberg Library, along with much more
information on the storm.

The State of Alabama Department of Archives and History,
through its director, Peter A. Brannon, furnished Civil War

data on Colonel C. D. Anderson, Sr., the keeper of Fort Point Lighthouse.

Published material was avoided unless it provided pertinent information not available elsewhere. One example is the story of Captain Rafferty and Battery O; much of this appeared in the November, 1900, *Cosmopolitan* in "The Galveston Tragedy," by John Fay.

The staff of the U. S. Weather Bureau office in Galveston, headed by Ernest Carson, made available every 1900 weather record in the office.

The library departments of the New Orleans *Times-Picayune* and the New Orleans *Item* furnished biographical information on Isaac Cline. (Much of the information about his brother, Joseph Cline, came from Mr. and Mrs. D. J. Cline—Joseph Cline's son and daughter-in-law—of Dallas.)

Both of the Clines wrote interesting autobiographies. Isaac Cline's was *Storms, Floods, and Sunshine* (Pelican Publishing Company, New Orleans, 1945). Joseph L. Cline's was *When the Heavens Frowned* (Mathis, Van Nort and Company, Dallas, 1946). Each devoted a chapter to the hurricane.

The two Clines had amazingly parallel careers. Both became highly respected Weather Bureau meteorologists.

From 1901 to 1935 Isaac Cline was in charge of the Weather Bureau office at New Orleans. In 1927 he predicted two weeks in advance the stages of a disastrous Mississippi River flood so accurately that Herbert Hoover, then Secretary of Commerce, cited him for the work.

Throughout his long career he was a meticulous weatherman; for example, he always insisted on using the term, "tropical cyclone," and frowned on the designation, "hurricane." But he also had a sense of humor.

"To avoid error," he enjoyed telling his New Orleans friends, "I keep an umbrella at both ends of the line."

Cline retired in 1935 after fifty-three years as a meteorologist; as a veteran of weather service since the days when it had been administered by the U. S. Army's Signal Corps, he was fond of saying, "I'm older than the Weather Bureau."

Joseph Cline left Galveston on November 14, 1900, to become sectional director for the Weather Bureau in Puerto Rico—a promotion given him in recognition of his work before and after the hurricane. Then, after service elsewhere, he had charge of the Dallas office for twenty-seven years. He retired in 1940, after forty-eight years with the Weather Bureau.

Clarence Ousley's *Galveston in 1900* (William C. Chase, 1900) is the most accurate of the books published during the year following the storm. Other interesting volumes—published later—on the city and the hurricane are *Galveston Community Book*, edited by Samuel Butler Graham (Arthur Cawston, 1945); *Hurricanes*, by I. R. Tannehill (Princeton University Press, 1945); *Meteorology*, by Willis Milham (Macmillan, 1912); the volumes of the *Monthly Weather Review for 1900*; *35,000 Days in Texas*, by Sam Acheson (Macmillan, 1938); and a master's thesis, *The Galveston Storm of 1900*, by Frank Thomas Harrowing (University of Houston, 1950).

Albert E. Smith, the newsreel photographer (who was later internationally known as the president of the Vitagraph Company in Hollywood), and Dr. William Crosthwait, who was in charge of William Randolph Hearst's relief train from Chicago, have written books in recent years. Each included a section on the storm. Mr. Smith's book was *Two Reels and a Crank* (Doubleday, 1952); Dr. Crosthwait's was *The Last Stitch* (Lippincott, 1956).

King Vidor's quotation is from a story, "Southern Storm," in the May, 1935, *Esquire*. The story was labeled fiction, but Mr. Vidor states that it is based on his recollection of the 1900 storm. (Vidor, incidentally, is not related to Charles Vidor, also a noted Hollywood director.)

Informational magazine articles are Walter Stevens' "The Story of the Galveston Disaster," *Munsey's*, December, 1900; Edwin Muller's "The Galveston Flood," *North American Review*, Winter, 1938; John Thomason, Jr.'s, "Catastrophe in Galveston," *American Mercury*, October, 1938.

I want to thank the following for their personal assistance. Many of these persons are survivors who tirelessly answered questions about their experiences in the storm and, later, read the appropriate parts of the manuscript for accuracy. Others are relatives of persons, now dead, who were in the storm; these people answered questions about their deceased relatives. Still others are experts, such as meteorologists, who provided information of a technical nature.

Mr. C. A. Anderson, meteorologist in charge, Waco, Texas, Weather Bureau office

Mr. A. J. Beckway, Galveston

Mr. and Mrs. Walter F. Bergstrom (she is the former Mary Lothringer), Galveston

Mr. Ronald Caskie, Galveston

Mr. E. R. Cheesborough, Galveston

Miss Madge Claiborne, Galveston

Mr. and Mrs. D. J. Cline, Dallas

Mrs. Tom Connally, Washington, D.C.

Mrs. Sarah Creson, Galveston

Dr. William L. Crosthwait, Waco, Texas

Mrs. H. M. Curtin and Ruth, Houston

Mr. Gordon E. Dunn, meteorologist in charge, Miami, Florida, Weather Bureau office

Mrs. F. H. Eastman (daughter of Edwin N. Ketchum), San Francisco, California

Dr. W. C. Fisher, Jr., Galveston

Mrs. Loraine S. Ford, Galveston

Mr. E. F. Gerloff, Galveston

Mrs. Joe Gilbert (the former Daisy Thorne), Austin, Texas

Miss Gertrude Girardeau, Galveston

Mr. D. Stuart Godwin, Jr., Houston

Miss Vida Godwin, Galveston

Mrs. Irene Goudge, Galveston

Mr. and Mrs. Walter Grover, Galveston

Mr. H. P. Hervey, Galveston

Mr. Bill Holman, Rosenberg Library, Galveston

Mrs. John W. Hopkins, Galveston

Mr. J. W. Jockusch, Jr., Galveston

Mr. Bee Jones, Galveston

Mr. Ralph Klaes, Galveston

Mr. I. H. Kempner, Galveston

Mr. Henry Ketchum, Galveston

Mr. Fred Langben, Galveston

Mr. Stephen Lichtblau, meteorologist in charge, New Orleans, Louisiana, Weather Bureau office

Mr. Thomas Loftus, Jr., Houston

Mr. and Mrs. Sydney Love, Galveston

Mrs. W. L. Love, Galveston

Mr. N. S. Lufkin, Galveston

Mr. G. J. Micheletti, chief, technical liaison branch, U. S. Army Corps of Engineers, Galveston

Miss Dorothy Minor, Galveston

Mr. and Mrs. Jens Moller, Jr., Galveston

Mr. James T. (Jim) Moore, Galveston

Mr. C. A. Paschetag, Galveston

Mr. Lee Paschetag, Galveston

Mr. Ben H. Peek, Hitchcock, Texas

Mr. R. H. Peek, Galveston

Mr. Charles Popular, Galveston

Dr. Edward Randall, Jr., Galveston

Mr. L. H. Runge, Jr., Galveston

Miss Betty Schmidt, Galveston

Dr. Zachary Scott, Austin, Texas

Mr. W. F. (Bill) Simpson, Sr., Groves, Texas

Mrs. W. S. Sinclair, Galveston

Mr. Young T. Sloan, meteorologist, Fort Worth, Texas, Weather Bureau office

Mr. Albert E. Smith, Los Angeles, California

Miss Mildred Stevenson, Rosenberg Library, Galveston

Mrs. J. J. Stumpf (the former Kate Hermann), Galveston

Mr. James G. Taylor, meteorologist, Galveston Weather Bureau office

Mrs. Francis Cline Drake Thompson (granddaughter of Isaac Cline), Metaire, Louisiana

Mr. and Mrs. N. C. Tobleman, Galveston

Mr. Jesse Toothaker, Galveston

Mr. and Mrs. George Trebosius (she is the former Florence Klaes), Galveston

Mrs. Charles Vidor, Los Angeles, California
Mr. King Vidor, Beverly Hills, California
Mrs. Frank Walker, Houston
Mrs. Z. L. White, Galveston
Mrs. William Whitridge, Houston
Mrs. Maud Mistrot Young, Galveston

INDEX